A Parent Guide to Hair Pulling Disorder

Effective Parenting Strategies for Children With Trichotillomania

(Formerly *Stay Out of My Hair!*)

by

Suzanne Mouton-Odum, Ph.D.
& Ruth Golomb, LCPC

Goldum Publishing

ISBN-10: 0615657400
ISBN-13: 9780615657400

Publisher's Note

This book is designed to provide information regarding the subject matter covered. It contains only the information available to the authors at the time of the printing. Furthermore, it is sold with the understanding that the authors and publisher are not engaged in rendering psychiatric, psychological, medical, or other professional services to the reader. If such services are required, they should be sought from a competent, licensed professional in the appropriate field.

Library of Congress Control Number: 2012949387

To our husbands and children
with love,
Brian, Alex, and Hayes
Jon, Nikki, and Jacob

Table of Contents

Acknowledgements

Thank you to Christina Pearson and the Trichotillomania Learning Center (TLC), for the endless support of the therapeutic work we do. The field of trichotillomania (trich, pronounced like *trick*) would still be in infancy if not for the tireless work of the TLC board, staff, and supporters. We are thankful for the community of professionals who have been united through the TLC, as well as the courageous sufferers who have been willing to share their stories, frustrations, and lives with us. Each one of you has influenced the scientific field, the development of clinical interventions, and us personally.

Thank you specifically to the families who were willing to share their stories with us for the purpose of this project. We believe that writing about real people and their unique histories lends an irreplaceable richness to the book. We know that the details you shared with us will undoubtedly enrich and heal others around the world that experience similar frustrations.

A special thanks to those individuals who read, gave feedback on, and helped to edit our book. Thank you to Mindi Stanley, Dave Keuler, Sherrie Vavricheck, Marty Franklin, Charley Mansueto, and Jonathan Golomb for sharing your knowledge and giving us unwavering support, enthusiasm, and encouragement in every step of this project. Finally, thank you to all of the professionals affiliated with the TLC. Just as individuals with trich feel isolated and disconnected from the mainstream, so too can we as professionals who are in the trenches. What a gift it is to be associated with so many wonderful and genuine people who have provided a warm, enthusiastic, professional home.

Introduction

This book initially began as a revision of *Stay Out of My Hair! Parenting Your Child with Trichotillomania*. However, we felt that so much has changed in the past four years, this new, improved version deserved a fresh name and a different look. Dealing with a child who struggles with hair pulling is frightening, frustrating, and confusing. Further, issues that parents of children with trich encounter are unique and profoundly different from those that parents of children with other conditions may face. As a result, parents are often more in need of support from a therapist than their child. As treatment providers who specialize in trich, we see hundreds of families affected by this disorder. Over the years, we have developed successful intervention programs for both children and their families and have distilled them into the pages of this book.

A Parent Guide to Hair Pulling Disorder will present up-to-date information about trichotillomania in a format that is relevant, understandable, validating, and interesting to you, a parent or caregiver of a child with trich. Our first goal is to help you understand how trich may affect your own emotions and/or reactions to your child and how it may affect the functioning of your family. Reading this book will also help you gain a better understanding of your child's experiences and your potential role in helping your child. Finally, we will offer concrete strategies to help you interact successfully with your child around hair pulling issues that will, in turn, improve your relationship with your child, change how your child views himself or herself, and ultimately result in decreased hair pulling behavior.

As therapeutic treatment providers, we believe that it is important to understand behavior in the context of a child's unique developmental process. In other words, when treating a three-year-old with trich, therapy will address developmental issues specific to three-year-olds. Accordingly, treatment of a twelve-year-old with trich will look different, even though therapy is based on similar principles and theoretical concepts.

To help our readers understand trichotillomania and relevant issues that are present at different developmental stages, we have selected four case examples to use throughout the book. We hope these cases will help you identify with parents who have encountered similar struggles. The cases are interwoven throughout the book to help demonstrate the use of specific strategies and interventions, as well as to illustrate the conceptualization and treatment of trichotillomania in children of different ages.

Additionally, we will help you understand your child's experiences in having trich to nurture compassion for your child. Growing up is hard enough, but growing up with trich complicates things. Understanding the normal developmental issues your child may be facing can help you tease out behaviors that are related to trichotillomania versus behaviors that are likely the result of normal development (that is, not everything is trich-related).

In sum, this book will provide you with an overview of what we, as researchers and clinicians, know about trichotillomania. It will introduce you to strategies for managing your own emotions so that your reactions to your child's pulling will be constructive and proactive. Finally, we will provide an overview of what treatment typically looks like, appropriate treatment expectations, your role in treatment, and specific ways that you, as a parent or caregiver, can be most helpful to your child and to the therapeutic process.

1

Tricho-what?
Understanding the Diagnosis

The History of Trich

The experience of parenting a child who pulls his or her own hair and is not able to stop can be frustrating, frightening, and very confusing, to say the least. Most parents have never heard of trichotillomania and have not ever considered pulling out their own hair. To many parents, the idea of pulling out one's hair seems bizarre, painful, or even pathological. Quite the contrary! Looking back through history, we see that hair pulling has been around for thousands of years and is more widespread than anyone ever suspected. The ancient Egyptians commonly used tweezers (as evidenced by their presence in archeological digs in Egypt), suggesting that they at least pulled hair for grooming. Further, there are references to hair pulling in both the Bible (book of Ezra) and Homer's *The Iliad.* Hippocrates, when describing how to interview a patient, wrote about routinely asking patients whether they pulled out their hair.

It was not until the late 1800s that trichotillomania got its name. A French dermatologist named Francois Henri Hallopeau was the first to describe hair pulling clinically and to give it a name. Trichotillomania is actually derived from the Greek roots *trich* meaning "hair," *tillo* meaning "pull" or "pulling," and *mania* meaning "out of control" or "frenzy." Literally, trichotillomania means "out of control hair pulling" or a "hair pulling frenzy."

Most people think hair pulling is a behavior driven by feelings of stress, anxiety, or being overwhelmed. When a person is feeling overwhelmed or stressed with life, he or she might say, "I could just pull my hair out!" What many people do not realize is that some individuals actually DO pull out their hair, whether it from stress or not.

What Is Trich?

The Diagnostic and Statistical Manual of the American Psychiatric Association (DSM-IV TR, 1994) categorizes trichotillomania as an Impulse Control Disorder defined by the following five criteria:

1. Repetitive pulling of one's own hair that results in noticeable hair loss;
2. A feeling of tension prior to pulling or when trying to resist the behavior;

3. Pleasure, gratification, or relief while engaging in the behavior;

4. The behavior is not accounted for by another medical (dermatological) or psychiatric problem (such as schizophrenia); and

5. The hair pulling leads to significant distress in one or more areas of the person's life (social, occupational, or work).

Although these criteria have been beneficial in describing a behavior that was not even been included in the Diagnostic and Statistical Manual, they are not adequate and will likely change in the next revision of it (DSM-V). Instead of classifying trich as an Impulse Control Disorder, it may be moved to Obsessive Compulsive Spectrum Disorders, a new classification for disorders that are compulsive but are not OCD proper. The diagnostic criteria for trichotillomania will likely change as well. After studying trich and working with hundreds of people who pull out their hair, we know that many people suffering with this problem do not meet all the old criteria. For example, some people pull hair from parts of their body that are not visible to others (pubic area, chest, arms, legs, and so on), so the hair loss cannot be seen. Even though the hair loss is not noticeable, it may still be a serious problem, causing shame, distress, or difficulty functioning in life (social, work, or family).

In addition, people report a variety of emotions other than tension prior to pulling, such as boredom, excitement, anger, frustration, guilt, and suspense. Others report that they really do not feel anything prior to pulling. In fact, many people are not even aware that they are having an urge to pull. Further, for many people hair pulling causes feelings of frustration, anger, and guilt, rather than pleasure or relief. Despite the diagnostic criteria being a bit limited, what we do know is that trichotillomania is a complex and unique problem that affects different people in different ways. In other words, although all people with trich pull hair, each person describes her pulling differently, and therefore treatment must be tailored to the individual.

Who Has Trich, and How Did My Child Get It?

So, how widespread is this seemingly rare and unheard-of disorder? Only a handful of studies have tried to estimate the prevalence of trich, so our understanding of the total number of people who pull their hair is limited at best. Dr. Gary Christenson and his colleagues at the University of Minnesota found that 1.5 percent of males and 3.4 percent of females in a college population met the criteria for trich as defined by the American Psychiatric Association in its 1994 manual. However, reports show much higher estimates for repetitive hair pulling that does not meet the full criteria for trich (without noticeable hair loss or with no reported tension-reduction cycle). For example, studies done by Dr. Melinda Stanley and Dr. Barbara Rothbaum demonstrate that despite traditional beliefs that hair pulling is both unusual and uncommon, repetitive hair pulling may affect as much as 10 to 22 percent of the population (tens of millions of people in the United States alone). These figures may make it easier to understand that your child is certainly not alone.

Most of the research regarding trichotillomania in the past thirty years has been with adults. However, recent studies conducted by Dr. Martin Franklin in Philadelphia have focused exclusively on children with trich. Interestingly, his results do not mirror what we see in adults. For example, the female-to-male ratio of trich in adults is 9:1, while in children, he found the female to male ratio to be 1:1. This means that for kids, hair pulling occurs in about the same number of boys as girls.

How do we account for this huge discrepancy? Is it that adult males with trich do not talk about it? Perhaps men pull from places that are not readily noticeable to the outside world, so the pulling does not cause them as many problems. Maybe they experience hair pulling as a problem, but they do not seek treatment. Perhaps more boys stop pulling during adolescence and therefore do not pull in adulthood. Because the average age of onset for trich is twelve to thirteen years of age (around puberty), it also is possible that the majority of people who begin pulling during puberty are female. As a result, the ratio switches sometime in adolescence to be predominantly female. Likely, it is some combination of all of these possibilities. Nevertheless, it is important to note that the same number of boys pull as girls.

The age at which children begin pulling has a wide range. Some children pull as early as six months of age, although more commonly repetitive hair pulling begins in early adolescence. In reality, however, children (and adults) can begin pulling at any age. No formula can determine the prognosis for children with trich (who will keep pulling into adulthood and who will stop) based on the age of onset.

Many health professionals tell parents that if a young child (less than five) begins to pull, he or she is likely to grow out of it. This is sometimes true, but not necessarily always the case. Upon hearing this, parents may decide to ignore the behavior (which is extremely difficult for most people) and perhaps not seek treatment that could benefit the parents and the child. This can be unfortunate for these children, because helping parents get appropriate information and guidance may enable the family to intervene early in order to change the pulling behavior.

Some children do seem to grow out of it—they pull for a time and eventually stop on their own. We do not know why some children are able to stop on their own and some struggle with pulling well into adulthood. We do know that children who receive good treatment early on are more likely to change their behavior.

Regardless of what age your child started pulling his or her hair, we believe it is important for you to educate yourself about trich and to follow the guidelines outlined in this book. In this way, you will better understand your child in the context of his or her development, manage your own emotions and reactions to your child's behavior, and identify specific ways to parent your child with trichotillomania successfully.

Shhh...It's a Secret

Despite the apparently widespread nature of trich, most people have never heard of it or believe that it is a rare phenomenon. Why is this? Why have most people heard of Tourette Syndrome or obsessive compulsive disorder, both of which are far less common than trich, but have never heard of hair pulling? The answer is complicated. First, most people with trich do not want to tell anyone about their behavior, because it is not widely talked about. Consequently, people with trich often believe that they are alone, thinking, *Surely no one else pulls out their own hair.* Unfortunately, raising awareness would require people with trich (or parents of children with trich) to talk about having the disorder—something that can be difficult to do.

Second, there is a great deal of shame surrounding hair pulling. Sufferers may be hesitant to talk about hair pulling because they are ashamed of it, perhaps largely because of the nature of the behavior—having bald spots that they themselves created. It is easier to talk about diabetes or asthma because these diseases or conditions are perceived to be out of a person's direct control. In the case of trich, however, there is a common perception that the person is causing the problem. But researchers have learned that brain processes can lead a person to pull hair. Hair pulling is not simply a choice but is likely biologically predetermined and requires energy, understanding, and professional help to change.

Misunderstandings about why people pull hair are common. In many cultures, hair represents beauty, youth, health, and strength. The systematic, noncosmetic removal of one's own hair can mistakenly imply a desire to be ugly or some underlying self-loathing or self-destructive tendency. These assumptions can further promote feelings of shame and humiliation. As a result of these faulty beliefs, people with trich are often blamed for their behavior. Because it is perceived to be under their control, people with trich are often told to "just quit doing it!" This kind of response is both blaming and unhelpful to the person suffering with trich. You can help your child by providing understanding and nurturing, particularly when your child hears blame, ridicule, or punishing statements from others. As you will learn in later chapters, children pull their hair because it feels good to them or helps them meet an intrinsic need, not because they want to be ugly or because they dislike themselves.

Emotional Problems In Addition To Trich

Often parents are concerned that if their child has trich, he or she also must have a serious underlying psychological difficulty or will eventually develop other, more serious psychological problems. Recent research on childhood trichotillomania conducted by Dr. Franklin and his colleagues shows that children with trich are no more likely to have another psychological disorder than children who don't have trich. However, findings from studies conducted with adults show that those with trich are more likely to suffer from depression and certain anxiety disorders, such as generalized anxiety disorder (excessive worry).

In other words, children with trich tend to be free of other psychological problems, while adults seem to suffer from more depression and anxiety. Why is this? We can hypothesize that if a person has struggled unsuccessfully for many years with trich, he or she may become depressed and/or feel overly anxious about certain areas of his or her life. This is probably the most important reason why we encourage parents to educate themselves and to intervene early in their child's life—to prevent suffering and hardship later. Supporting and nurturing your child will encourage the development of a positive self-image and greater self-worth.

Studies have demonstrated that there is a higher rate of certain psychological disorders among family members of individuals with trich. Family members of people with trich are more likely to have a diagnosis of trich, obsessive compulsive disorder, Tourette Syndrome, anxiety disorders, major depression, and other body-focused repetitive behaviors (BFRBs), such as skin picking, nail biting, thumb sucking, cheek or lip biting, cuticle picking, or tooth grinding. Often, at the first therapy session parents will say something like *No one in our family has ever done anything like this*, while at the same time they are biting their nails. Parents who are self-aware and take time to examine their own habits and behaviors are better able to develop empathy for their child and his or her experiences.

Sometimes when talking to parents, we use examples of habits that are hard to change that they might better relate to, like overeating or smoking. For example, have you ever ordered a hamburger instead of a salad, knowing that the salad would be healthier? Have you ever tried to quit smoking or to give up caffeine?

With this in mind, take a minute to consider any behaviors that you or your family members engage in that are both unhealthy and difficult to change. Does anyone in your family or your spouse's family bite their fingernails, bite their lip or the inside of their cheek, pick their cuticles, fingernails, or skin (acne, mosquito bites, scabs, calluses), overeat, smoke, or crack their knuckles? More than likely they do. Have you ever tried to change any of these behaviors yourself? If so, was it difficult? Were you successful? Was it ever frustrating for you to make these changes? Did you ever experience failure?

Are you starting to understand? Although these behaviors can be more socially acceptable and may not result in the same type of physical damage, they are similar to trich in that they are all under the umbrella of BFRBs and are hard behaviors to change. If you have ever tried, you know first-hand that it is not easy to break a habit. Behavior change requires education, motivation, readiness, energy, hard work, and support from those around you.

Is Trich Self-Mutilation?

The public misunderstands trichotillomania tremendously. Recent Internet postings state that hair pulling is in the same category as, or ultimately leads to, self-injurious cutting commonly referred to as "self-mutilation." There is no scientific data to support this assertion and, in fact, trich and self-mutilation seem to involve quite different processes. People who pull out their hair do it because some aspect of it feels good, not because they want to harm or disfigure themselves. People who cut or otherwise injure themselves often describe wanting to feel physical pain as opposed to emotional pain. The self-injury may help them to "drown out" the emotional pain. In other words, the processes underlying each may be completely different; thus, we would argue that they are categorically different behaviors. Therefore, hair pulling is not a form of nor will it lead to cutting or other forms of self-mutilation.

Is My Child Trying to Manipulate Me or "Get Back At Me" by Pulling?

Over the years, we have had parents ask if their child "pulls to get back at me," suggesting that maybe this is not trich, but an oppositional or defiant behavior. The answer is no. Children do not develop a disfiguring disorder that is shrouded in shame and secrecy to get back at you. However, the dynamic of pulling to get back at a parent could develop (particularly in adolescence), but this dynamic is not what is causing the hair pulling. If this sounds familiar to you, understand that there is a dynamic between you and your child at play and that a large component of helping your child is to change your part of this interaction. Think about two people doing a dance. Maybe you are both doing a waltz. As long as both people are doing the appropriate waltz steps, everything keeps going nicely. If one of you (usually the parent) changes the dance and starts to jitterbug, the dance must change (or it could get confusing). Once you change your behavior, it has a profound impact on what your child does and his or her former behavior is no longer possible—that is, it is impossible to waltz when your dance partner is doing the jitterbug. We will discuss this dynamic in adolescents in detail in chapter six.

Who Is Motivated: You or Your Child?

Frequently, individuals come to treatment stating, "I really want to stop pulling my hair." Upon further investigation by a trained therapist, these individuals often admit that they do not really want to stop pulling, but desire to grow back their hair, so they feel like they should stop. In other words, people like to pull hair, but they do not like the outcome of pulling (bald patches or thinning of the hair). Simply put, for many people hair pulling feels good. A parallel example might be "I like eating chocolate cake, but I do not like the way it makes me feel or look. Sometimes, though, I still choose to eat it, even though I know it will cause me to gain weight." This ambivalence is something that most of us can relate to and helps us understand the complex feelings that a child may experience when pulling hair.

When working with a child, it is especially important to gauge the child's level of ambivalence or confusion about changing his or her behavior. It is possible that you are more motivated than your child is to change the behavior. These feelings can be confusing to your child and very frustrating for you. How both the therapist and parents handle these complicated situations can have a significant impact on the parent-child relationship and on the ultimate success of the therapy. Chapters four and five will provide specific tools for you to better understand your child's feelings about having trich, as well as strategies for helping him or her to feel less confused and more empowered to change.

Trich as a Part of a Larger Class of Disorders: Body-Focused Repetitive Behaviors

Trich may be under a larger umbrella of related disorders we refer to as body-focused repetitive behaviors (BFRBs). As mentioned earlier, examples of other BFRBs include nail biting, thumb sucking, skin picking, lip biting, cheek biting, cuticle picking, nail picking, tooth grinding, and knuckle cracking. These behaviors are often thought of as simple "nervous habits." The term *habit* implies there is something simple about stopping the behavior. However, if you look at another "habit" you see that most people with that habit require some type of help to quit.

Consider, for example, overeating, smoking, or gambling. Most people who overeat, smoke, or gamble compulsively require some type of professional or organized help—sometimes extensive help—to deal adequately with these behaviors. However, if you have ever tried to stop doing a BFRB, you know that the behavior is neither simple nor easily discarded. As stated earlier in this chapter, it is common for people who have trich to have one or more of the other BFRBs. What we know about BFRBs is that they are more than just "bad habits"; they are complex, biologically based behaviors that are started and reinforced by many internal (physiological) and external (environmental) forces. We will discuss all of these "forces" in chapter seven, as well as how therapy can specifically address them.

Is Trich the Result of Trauma?

Some people mistakenly assume that children begin to pull out their hair as the result of a traumatic or negative event. Therapists who think this way are inspired by the school of psychoanalysis that teaches that behaviors and anxieties are manifestations of deeper, unresolved issues from childhood that creep up from the subconscious into the conscious life. However, only 50 percent of people with trich report a negative event occurring at the time their hair pulling began. Negative events can be such common occurrences as moving to a new town, changing schools, parents divorcing, or losing a friend. The other 50 percent report no stressor at the time hair pulling began. Indeed, some of the "stressors" mentioned are common occurrences in growing up. Thus, it is erroneous to assume that trich is the result of a negative or stressful event that your child has experienced but perhaps not verbalized.

How Genes Play a Part

Research has not yet demonstrated why hair pulling manifests in one person and not in another. There seems to be a family correlation with trich, meaning that if one person in the family has trich, there is a higher likelihood that another person will also have it. However, we see cases all the time where a child has trichotillomania, but there seems to be no other person in the family who suffers from it. When we look at the incidence of other BFRBs in the families of people with trich, we see a higher correlation. In other words, although no one else in the family may pull hair, some relative (perhaps distant) may bite their nails or pick skin, thus engaging in another BFRB. As stated earlier, hair pulling may be part of this larger category of behaviors.

Not only do we see a higher incidence of BFRBs in family members of people with trich, we also see a higher incidence of them in people who have trich. Up to 40 percent of people who pull hair also engage in some type of skin picking behavior. As a result, treatment of trichotillomania often includes the treatment of other BFRBs as well. A recent study by Dr. Carol Novak examined hair pulling in identical and fraternal twins. This study reported that there is higher incidence of hair pulling in identical twins than in fraternal twins, which resembles other genetically based disorders. Thus, she discovered that a significant component in trich is inherited.

Hair Pulling Severity: What Does Trich Look Like?

Many parents initially perceive any hair pulling as severe, simply because it is outside their normal experience. Some parents find it helpful to see different severities of pulling, to gain needed perspective of just where their child is in the development of the disorder. It is difficult to "rate" hair pulling as mild, moderate, and severe, as different treatment providers have varied opinions on this subject. Having treated hundreds of people with trich, we have witnessed a wide range of pulling severity as depicted in the following pictures.

With regard to eyelash and eyebrow pulling, it is important to note that significant denuding of the area can happen even though fewer hairs have been pulled, simply because there are fewer hairs in these areas. Whereas pulling fifty hairs on the scalp may result in no noticeable hair loss, this same number of hairs pulled on the eyelid would likely result in noticeable hair loss.

Mild hair loss

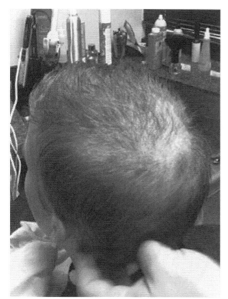
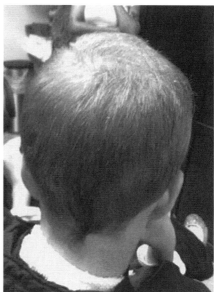

Moderate hair loss

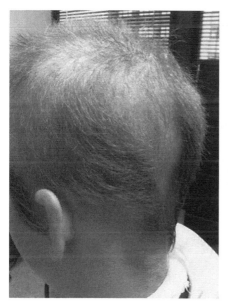
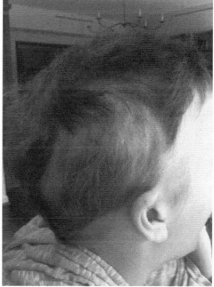

Severe hair loss

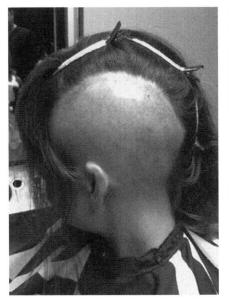 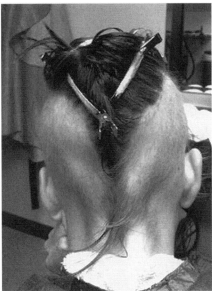

Common Theories about Trich

To understand trichotillomania and the various theories that have been used to describe the behavior, it is useful to take an historical perspective. As mentioned earlier, one of the first theories describing trichotillomania was the psychoanalytic theory. In keeping with this perspective, trich was initially described as the result of a trauma or an unresolved psychosexual issue that manifested in pulling behavior. Therefore, treatment was aimed at resolving the "issue," thus eliminating the need to pull. What therapists trained in this theory ultimately learned was that despite such issues being resolved, the hair pulling behavior itself often remained constant. Also, many people came for treatment with relatively few issues and described a normal, loving, uneventful childhood experience. As a result, new theories began to arise to describe the onset and course of hair pulling behavior.

Trichotillomania also has been understood to be a disorder of habit. This theory, developed by Nathan Azrin and R. Gregory Nunn, serves as the basis for a treatment called Habit Reversal Training (HRT). The theory posits that hair pulling begins spontaneously or is learned, then becomes associated with a variety of cues and contexts that perpetuate the behavior. For example, if a person pulls his or her hair every time he or she talks on the phone, pulling or thinking of pulling becomes a habit when the phone is raised to the ear. So, those who pull hair are taught strategies that "compete" with hair pulling behavior in such situations. In addition, other strategies, such as relaxation training, contingency management, and social support, are offered. Although this theory does a good job of explaining and addressing certain aspects of hair pulling behavior, it does not adequately describe the entire spectrum of hair pulling triggers and cues.

Theorists also have looked to the animal world to understand trichotillomania. We often see pulling or plucking behavior in cats, dogs, monkeys, birds, and mice. It is unclear, however, whether a bird that plucks her feathers or a monkey that pulls his fur actually has trichotillomania. Recently, scientists have identified the part of the genetic code in mice that, when mutated, causes the offspring of that mouse to chew its fur off. This breakthrough caused many people to become interested in the possibility of finding a genetic cause for trich, which may ultimately lead to a cure. However, although hair pulling behavior appears to be similar in animals, researchers cannot be sure that the behavior observed in these animals is indeed trichotillomania. Nonetheless, this research is both exciting and ground breaking, and it will likely contribute to the science of understanding trichotillomania.

Cognitive behavioral psychologists have applied their theory to trich and have been more comprehensive in explaining and understanding hair pulling behavior. In fact, this book focuses on the principles of Cognitive Behavioral Therapy (CBT) that explain and guide the treatment of trichotillomania. This therapy integrates a person's beliefs or thoughts (cognitions) with behavioral experiences, such as positive reinforcers (that is, it feels good) or negative reinforcers (that is, it makes bad feelings go away) to explain why a behavior begins and persists.

Dr. Charles Mansueto and his colleagues at the Behavior Therapy Center of Greater Washington have utilized the principles of CBT to expand the earlier work of Habit Reversal Therapy as it applies to trichotillomania. Dr. Mansueto's approach is referred to as the Comprehensive Behavioral Model, or ComB Model. Therapists utilizing the ComB Model evaluate a person's unique cognitive and behavioral experiences to develop a *behavioral analysis* or *functional analysis* to explain what purpose the hair pulling serves for that individual. As stated earlier, people pull hair because some aspect of it "feels good" or otherwise helps them meet certain needs. This comprehensive analysis informs the therapist as to how hair pulling helps the individual meet these needs, which then opens the door to finding individualized coping strategies to help that person to stop pulling.

Many components contribute to the development of behavioral patterns that may result in hair pulling behavior. These components include:

1. Sensory experiences before, during, and after the pulling process;
2. Cognitions or thoughts about hair, hair pulling, and what the person thinks will happen if hair is not pulled;
3. Emotional experiences before, during, and after hair pulling;
4. Motor behaviors, such as mindlessly stroking one's hair either before or after the hair is pulled; and
5. Environmental cues and triggers (common places and activities where hair pulling tends to occur).

In gathering all this information, a trained therapist is able to create a more comprehensive understanding of why a person pulls his or her hair and, more importantly, how best to help manage that behavior. We will discuss these concepts at length in chapter seven.

Now that we have given you a bit of history, answered some common questions, and reviewed several theories about trichotillomania, we are going to describe several case examples of children with trichotillomania. In the next chapter, we will illustrate how hair pulling can uniquely affect children and their families at different stages of development.

2

What is Happening to My Child?

Now that we have reviewed the history of and literature about trichotillomania, let's look at some examples of families dealing with a child who has trich. Some of these situations may sound familiar to you, while others may be very different from yours.

In the Beginning

Ashley

"I always thought it was cute the way little Ashley sucked her thumb and twirled her hair. She had been doing that for as long as I could remember. Sometimes she would even twirl my hair! But when she was about two, I noticed a bald spot where she twirled her hair. Soon the bald spot spread,

and I noticed that she was pulling out her hair and twisting it around her thumb while she sucked. Was I doing something wrong? Was I causing her to pull out her hair? At first I freaked out. I started to tell her 'No!' when she even touched her head. I lectured, I bribed, I cried, I punished, and I yelled."

Charles and Jane are Ashley's parents. Like many parents, they experienced a wide range of emotions when they first realized that Ashley was pulling out her hair. Being a parent is the most rewarding, perplexing, wonderful, confusing, and humbling job any of us will ever have. As a result, we put a lot of pressure on ourselves to be good (dare we say "perfect") parents. Unfortunately, there is no such thing. In addition, this is one job without a job description, and every good parent does it differently.

So, what is a parent to do when a child has a problem? Many times parents react with fear, understandably. The fear response (particularly when the fear pertains to the protection of offspring) is intense and driven by adrenaline. The hard-wired, immediate reaction is to do whatever is necessary to "protect" the offspring. In humans, when a child is pulling hair, this fear response is activated and can cause immediate, action-oriented parent responses. Know that these responses are normal and biologically driven. Now that you have had some time to process this behavior (and have probably experienced a variety of other emotions, such as frustration, confusion, guilt and even anger), it is time to turn your attention toward education.

The first step in educating yourself is to obtain good information (you have started doing this by reading this book) about trichotillomania. Talk to your child's pediatrician to make sure that your child's hair loss is due to pulling and not some other condition. Join the Trichotillomania Learning Center (a national organization that helps drive serious research in the trich field, raises public awareness, and helps individuals and families to obtain good information and to connect with others who have the same problem).

Find out exactly what is going on and begin to formulate a plan. When you are the parent of a toddler or preschool-aged child, much of the work is going to be guided by you (two-year-olds aren't at all introspective). It is important to listen to information that is given to you and to be willing to try some things at home. Finally, it is always helpful to feel supported, to have good guidance, and to begin to understand that you did not "cause" this behavior and that you are a crucial part of the healing process. As we will outline throughout this book, you will be an active part of the treatment process, with your direct involvement varying depending on the age of your child.

Interventions for toddlers and preschoolers are different from those for older children. It's all up to you to learn how to help, support, reinforce, and modify behavior. Just as you support and guide your child at this stage by deciding when to start potty training, to give up the pacifier, or to transition out of a crib into a bed, you need to use the same parenting skills to address hair pulling. You will be the guiding force for your child at this stage of development.

Fortunately, toddlers and preschoolers are developing and changing so rapidly that understanding how *not* to pull hair is just one other thing that the child is learning while growing up. Therefore, you need to be committed to the process and have energy to deal with the inevitable ups and downs as you help your child develop strategies to change his or her behavior. And who knows? You may find that this is a wonderful opportunity to change some aspect of your own behavior. Many times when parents change their behavior (for example, being more positive and less focused on hair pulling), it can affect the child's behavior, without the child even realizing why his or her behavior has changed. Also, if this is not a good time for you to devote time and energy to helping your child change hair pulling behavior, don't. You can always work on it later, when you have adequate time and energy. Consider trying to ignore the behavior for a few months and see if it improves on its own. (Be aware that ignoring behavior is much harder than it sounds. But it's a reasonable thing to try.) Sometimes simply letting go of trying to control the child's behavior gives you and your child space to breathe and to begin to heal.

Why My Child?

Sarah

"Sarah came home from her second-grade class one day missing all of her eyelashes on one eye. I was shocked. I asked her in a panic, 'What happened?' Sarah did not respond at all. When she finally did, she seemed completely confused about my question. All she said is, 'What are you talking about?' Over the next few days, all of her eyelashes disappeared. I became increasingly worried. Sarah promised me that she had no idea what I was talking about. She noticed that eyelashes were gone, but said she had *absolutely no idea what had happened. How could this be? Is she sick? Is she completely out of touch with reality? What kind of a doctor should I bring her to? Help!"*

Stu and Karen, Sarah's parents, quickly became worried and confused. Since Sarah seemed unaware of what happened to her eyelashes, they wondered what was wrong with her. And they did not know where to turn. "Why is this happening?" and "What is happening?" were the two thoughts that kept turning around and around in Karen's head.

Sarah has trichotillomania. While she was actually oblivious to her behavior and unconcerned about her hair loss, her parents' reactions surprised and upset her. Stu and Karen were so shocked when Sarah came home from school with no eyelashes on one eye that they raised their voices and loudly interrogated her. Sarah became upset and embarrassed, and she did not know how to talk to her parents about it.

Sarah is a very responsible, high-achieving child. She feels as if she is doing something wrong, and at the same time, she can't stop herself. Most of all she feels shame—shame that she is creating this problem that is upsetting the family. It is the worst feeling in the world for her. Sarah continues to tell her parents that she has no idea what happened to her eyelashes, because telling them the truth would be ten times worse. They are already upset enough.

Stu and Karen start to feel strongly that Sarah is purposely lying to them. How can she truly not know what she is doing? They have walked into the room and seen her pulling at her eyelashes. Stu and Karen wonder what is happening to their precious daughter that would turn her into what they perceive to be a lying, deceitful person.

This is a very challenging situation for any parent. Adding to the distress is the idea that your child may be hurting herself *and* lying. Understanding your child's point of view may be very helpful. Children who pull their hair are good kids who have found a unique and powerful way to soothe themselves. Often kids truly don't know why they pull; however, they do know that it feels good. Similar to when a mosquito bites you and you automatically scratch to make it feel better, children can pull to relieve a sensation without even realizing it. So, it's hard to say whether these children "want" to pull. On one hand, they do, because it feels good. On the other hand, they don't, because they don't like to upset the family or they don't like the results of pulling—hair loss and feeling badly about themselves. Trich is a complicated problem at this stage. Therefore, to maintain the feeling of being a good person and to avoid further upset, children often say that they are "not pulling" or that they "don't know how the hair came out."

It is important to provide a calm, safe environment for children to feel comfortable exploring the possibility that they might be pulling out their hair. It helps to take a matter-of-fact approach. Providing understandable information about this interesting behavior called trichotillomania, which means hair pulling, is a good way to start. Talk openly with your child, and try not judge or blame him or her. In addition, provide information a little at a time to give your child time to digest it slowly and effectively. The first time that you sit down to talk about trich, you may be the only one talking. At this sitting, consider giving only one or two small pieces of information, such as "lots of kids pull out their hair" and "children pull their hair because it feels good to them."

Most importantly, if you do only one thing during this first conversation, express to your child that you love him or her no matter what. Make it clear that hair pulling is not a determining factor of your child's goodness as a human being. Your child will be tremendously relieved, and it will take off some of the pressure of wondering if you are still going to love and support him or her.

Many parents think that accepting trich in their child is somehow condoning the behavior and therefore prolonging it. We have not found this to be true at all. Parents who take a loving approach with their children and their children's trich find that they, and their children, navigate the recovery process much more easily than those who take a more punitive, unsupportive, or negative approach.

Common Mistaken Beliefs

Hannah

One day Hannah came downstairs crying and said, "I can't cover this spot anymore!" "What spot?" Peggy asked. This was the beginning of a long, hard journey. Peggy wondered what was going on in school that was causing Hannah to pull out her hair. And worse, why would she pull out her pubic hair? Does she not want to become a woman? Is she ashamed of growing up?

Middle school is a tough time for parents in the best of circumstances, but for Peggy and Bob it became a nightmare. Hannah started to pull hair out of her scalp and pubic area when she was twelve. Peggy noticed that Hannah was spending more time in the bathroom in the morning. She thought that Hannah was just being a teenager and fussing with her hair.

Peggy knew that being twelve years old is a tough time, but really! What is so bad that is causing Hannah to pull out her hair? Hannah had stopped confiding in Peggy a few years before, as she began to approach adolescence, so although Peggy knew her friends and teachers, she did not really know what was going on in Hannah's head from day to day. Was being a good student too much pressure? Were they, as her parents, expecting too much from her?

Peggy and Bob made an appointment with the school counselor and Hannah's teachers. To their amazement, the teachers and the counselor had no idea that Hannah was struggling, unhappy, or pulling out her hair. They had never heard of such a thing and suggested rather judgmentally that something must be wrong at home. The counselor spoke privately with the parents after the meeting and warned Peggy and Bob that the behavior was a form of self-mutilation and that the next step for Hannah would likely be to start cutting herself.

After the meeting, Peggy and Bob were absolutely beside themselves. What were they doing that was causing their child to hurt herself? Had someone abused her? Hannah seemed like a happy, well-adjusted teen. Could they be that out of touch? Peggy called the pediatrician and made an emergency appointment. After speaking with Hannah, the pediatrician concluded that this was "just a phase" and that she would simply grow out of it. He told them that if Hannah did not grow out of it in the next few months, Peggy and Bob were not to tolerate the behavior and were to punish her every time she pulled her hair.

Now Peggy and Bob were very confused. What should they do? Should they treat this as self-mutilation and possibly hospitalize her? Should they ignore it and hope it goes away? Or should they punish her for pulling? Many parents receive very conflicting recommendations. Finding a reliable source of information can be extremely challenging. All Peggy and Bob want is what is best for Hannah, but what is best for her?

How can parents find a reliable source of information? Isn't the school a good source? And surely a pediatrician would know about trichotillomania. Unfortunately, many pediatricians have only a cursory understanding of trichotillomania and, depending on how recently your pediatrician graduated from medical school, his or her information may be outdated. Well-meaning professionals sometimes are not current on all the reliable information available to them.

When dealing with trich, it is important to consult with an expert—someone who has experience working with people who have this problem. In today's health-care system, a doctor with a specialty is usually the first stop, not the last. If you have allergies, you consult an allergist; heart problems, a cardiologist; asthma, a pulmonologist; and so on. When your child is pulling out hair, whom should you consult?

A good place to start is with the previously mentioned Trichotillomania Learning Center (TLC; www.trich.org), a national nonprofit organization located in Santa Cruz, California. The TLC has much useful information, including brochures and resources for schools, cosmetologists, and doctors, as well as lists of therapists throughout the country who are trained to work with adults and children with trich. When you contact a professional (such as the school counselor or pediatrician), ask how many children he or she has seen with this problem and how much success he or she has had with treatment. It is important to know that the person you select has good knowledge and training in working with children who pull out their hair.

You may already have consulted with a professional and received some mistaken information. If this is the case, you are not alone. No matter what people have told you, here are some important things to remember:

1. Hair pulling is not a symptom of an underlying problem or emotional disorder; most children who pull their hair are quite happy, well-adjusted individuals.

2. Although some kids do stop pulling on their own, some do not. If possible, early intervention can be very helpful and is advisable.

3. Children pull because it helps them feel better in some way or meets a need. The behavior is *not* self-abuse or an indication of self-loathing, low self-esteem, or an underlying psychological disturbance.

4. Hair pulling is not a result of sexual abuse, trauma, or a harmful past experience. If that were the case, all victims of sexual abuse would pull out their hair. Any stressful event can be a catalyst for trich if the predisposition is there. But sometimes there is no observable catalyst at all.

5. Hair pulling does not predict the future onset of anything (including self-mutilation, depression, anxiety, or obsessive compulsive disorder).

6. Hair pulling is not a sign of self-hatred or a desire to be ugly. (However, left untreated, these feelings can occur because of years of performing a perplexing behavior and feeling isolated and out of control.)

7. Hair pulling is not an easy behavior to stop without assistance. Simply telling your child "Stop it" or "You would stop doing it if you really wanted to" feels blaming and unsupportive to him or her.

8. Punishing your child for pulling hair is never a good solution, as it is invalidating, fosters low self-esteem, and instills shame. In addition, negative parent reactions to hair pulling may lead a child to hide his or her behavior and to develop techniques for deflection and lying, simply to avoid punishment.

Is It My Fault? What Did I Do Wrong?

Hayden

When Ellen first looked closely at her son Hayden's hair loss, it was substantial, covering most of his crown and the sides of his scalp with only a thin layer of hair veiling the bald spot. When Ellen anxiously asked about the hair loss, Hayden said, "It's nothing, Mom. Don't worry about it." Ellen remembered that when Hayden was going into kindergarten, he had some bald patches, but the hair grew back by winter break, and he never had another problem. She had chalked this up to alopecia and never sought treatment, but this seemed different, more severe.

Hayden is in the tenth grade and has always been a shy, introspective child. He is artistic, creative, and very smart. He is the "hero child" of the family, always trying to do his personal best to impress his parents and get positive feedback from them. He is the first-born of three children and has always protected and watched over his younger siblings.

His parents, Ellen and Fred, are loving and supportive of Hayden, but recently decided to separate due to longstanding marital conflict. Although they did their best to keep their three children out of marital issues and discussions, sometimes Hayden was able to hear arguments late at night when they were less vigilant of their voice tone.

At sixteen, Hayden began to pull out his scalp hair. Because he had always been so quiet and did not share many feelings with his parents, the pulling went unnoticed for some time. Further, because he has always focused on "doing good," he was especially reticent to tell his parents what was going on.

At first, Ellen and Fred began to blame themselves, feeling responsible for Hayden's behavior as they were causing the divorce and thus causing the stress. Later they began to blame each other, using Hayden's pulling as a weapon to find fault with each other's parenting abilities. For example, when Hayden returned from visits with his father, if Ellen noticed any hair loss, she immediately attributed it to "stress at Dad's house," lending support to her argument that her former husband was "unfit."

It's important to understand that children whose parents go through a divorce have complicated feelings. But most children who experience divorce in the family do not pull out their hair. At the same time, many children from happy, intact families do pull out their hair. Therefore, assuming divorce is a cause for hair pulling is unfounded.

Children start pulling out their hair for reasons that can but don't necessarily include stress, abuse, or trauma. If a child has a predisposition to hair pulling, stress can absolutely lead a child to "discover" her hair. But in many cases, normal life events can "trigger" hair pulling. Some precipitating events outside of trauma, abuse, or life stress include but are not limited to:

1. Examining a hair pulled from one's head under a microscope in science class;
2. Giving an eyelash as a "ticket" to join a group of friends at play;
3. Making a wish on an eyelash;
4. Pulling a stray or errant hair out during grooming, which can awaken the desire to pull more; and

5. Seeing another child pull (maybe one who is popular or highly respected).

Any of these common and innocent events can set the stage for hair pulling. It is a mistake to assume that because a child pulls her hair she is the victim of trauma or abuse. But it is important to examine different aspects in your child's life. Talk to her, gather information about events going on at school, and investigate to see if there is an important issue that you are not aware of, one that she may need help with. As with any challenging behavior, stress can both exacerbate it and make it more difficult to manage.

It is also important to remember that your child's pulling is not your fault, and in the case of Hayden, it is not either parent's fault. As parents, we tend to blame ourselves when things don't go the way we think they should. Hair pulling can become a way of coping with unpleasant emotions for some children, but that is not always the case. For Hayden, pulling may have happened in response to feelings of stress about his parents' divorce, or it simply may have developed over time, or some combination of the two. We cannot assume that it is either. A careful evaluation by a trained therapist is necessary to determine how this behavior is meeting your child's needs. Then a treatment plan to address these needs will need to be developed.

As you have seen, each child has a unique experience with hair pulling and his or her family circumstances. Developmental stages, maturity, and family situations all contribute to the overall impact that trichotillomania has on the child and the family. In the next chapter, we will explore the emotional toll trichotillomania can have on parents.

3

Common Feelings and Reactions Parents Experience

This Feels Horrible!

Most parents who discover that their children are pulling their hair initially feel scared. It's unsettling at best to see your child engage in a behavior that seems so odd and unfamiliar to you. In addition, the resulting bald spot draws unwanted attention to your child and ultimately to you. The unspoken reaction from others may be perceived as (in many cases accurately), "What in heaven's name are you doing at home that is causing your child to pull out his [or her] hair?" or "You must be an awful parent." Even if others aren't thinking this, very often moms and dads are thinking it about themselves. It feels absolutely awful. Most parents initially report feeling extremely frustrated and hopeless because they lack the skills and information to be able to change this confusing behavior.

Parents frequently feel angry with their children for doing this to themselves and angry with themselves for being helpless. These feelings can also make parents feel lonely. Most parents have difficulty talking about it with other people. After all, what are others going to think? *I already feel like the worst parent in the world; I don't need someone else telling me that.* So, many parents keep the information to themselves and feel isolated.

Worst of all, parents can feel ashamed of their child for the way he or she looks. They find themselves wanting to cover the hair loss to avoid their own embarrassment and shame about how their child looks, even when the child does not care. All these feelings are normal and common reactions to dealing with a child who has trich. Before we try to cope with these feelings, let's try to understand a little more about trich and about what you are dealing with.

Getting Ready

As stated in chapter one, trich is a complex behavior that manifests itself a little differently for each person. A trained psychologist or other mental health provider knows that it is valuable to evaluate a child's behavior completely before formulating a comprehensive behavioral treatment plan. But many parents find it hard to understand that the process of change takes time. Often, parents take their child to therapy and expect specific techniques up front during that first session. The therapist can offer some strategies then, but a thorough evaluation is necessary before he or she can identify and offer specific, tailored strategies. In other words, be patient. It is important for your child's therapist to develop a trusting relationship with your child and to understand fully how hair pulling works for him or her.

Getting your child ready to participate in treatment may also take time. As stated earlier, parents are often motivated for therapy, but the child is likely ambivalent. It can take several sessions of working with a child to get him or her to the point of readiness—and sometimes it takes longer. Have you ever been told that you should lose weight and *not* gone out the next day and started a program of weight loss? Have you ever joined a health club and not gone to work out there? Sometimes it takes weeks, months, or even years before a child is at the point of saying, "Okay, I am ready to do this." Understand that your child may not be at the point of readiness at the same time you are. Give your child time to get there. If you are patient and can wait until he or she is ready, the treatment will be much more successful than if you push the process.

All four of our cases include parents who are more motivated for change than their children. As a result, these parents experience common pitfalls and make mistakes that happen all too often in the case of childhood and adolescent trich. Let's see how each of them proceeds along their course of treatment.

Ignoring Behavior Is Harder Than You Think

Ashley

Ashley's parents decided to take her to the pediatrician to address her pulling while sucking her thumb. The doctor recommended that they ignore the behavior. Charles and Jane made every effort to ignore it. But when Ashley sucked her thumb and pulled her hair, Jane got upset. She didn't say anything *directly*; instead she said things like, "You want your hair to grow nice and long so we can put it into a pretty ponytail, don't you?" and "Look at Dora the Explorer's pretty hair. You want your hair to look like that, right?" Since Jane was not commenting on the pulling, she thought she was doing a good job of ignoring the behavior. However, she also became visibly upset and teary sometimes. At other times, she abruptly left the room to cry. Ashley was confused and upset. She didn't understand why her mother was so sad, but she did know that she was the cause.

Charles was usually gone during work hours, so he did not witness Ashley's daytime pulling. When he got home, he spent a lot of time trying to comfort Jane. He was very frustrated because he could not "fix" the problem and make his family feel good, like they used to feel.

When he put Ashley to bed, he simply pulled her hands down whenever they crept up to her head. This frustrated Ashley. She cried and sometimes tried to hit Charles when he moved her hands. He tried putting socks on her hands, but she promptly took them off. Charles became aggravated, and he eventually avoided tucking Ashley into bed altogether.

Charles and Jane thought, *What a mess! This ignoring is definitely not working.* Well, we agree that their attempts were not working, but Charles and Jane also were not ignoring the behavior. Just the opposite: they were paying *close* attention to the behavior and had *very* strong reactions.

All children, particularly young children, are exquisitely tuned in to their parents' reactions to them. Children find it extremely interesting to watch their parents react because of their behavior. They may not know exactly what mom is feeling, but they know that something is up; Mom is upset. Being able to control a parent's emotions makes a child feel powerful. Sometimes this is fun for children, but other times it's confusing or even frightening. Often children don't want that much power. However, they do want and need attention. And if they can't get positive attention, any attention will do. In addition, hair pulling felt good to Ashley—most of the time she was pulling simply because it soothed her. She was confused to see her parents get upset when she was doing something that felt good.

It is extremely difficult to ignore an unwanted behavior in your child. Ignoring behavior means not responding to it *at all*. No comments about hair, no comments about other people's hair, no heavy sighs, no attempts to stop the behavior—nothing. For many parents (if not all), ignoring hair pulling behavior is almost impossible. If you feel that you cannot truly ignore it, don't even try—ask for another suggestion.

Patience with yourself and your child is critical at this stage. You must be patient when deciding which suggestions make sense for you and your family, as well as when to try out different intervention ideas. Trying something and determining that it won't work for you is as important as finding out what does work. For Charles and Jane, ignoring is not a workable strategy. If the pediatrician has nothing more to offer, seek guidance elsewhere.

The Blame Game

Sarah

Stu and Karen, the parents of second-grade Sarah, took her to see a dermatologist, as they thought that perhaps a skin disorder was causing her eyelashes and eyebrows to fall out. The dermatologist determined that the hairs had been plucked and that trichotillomania, not alopecia, was the diagnosis. The family was referred to a therapist who knew about behavior therapy but had never heard about trichotillomania.

At first, Sarah did not even want to talk to the therapist. She was completely unwilling to discuss hair or hair pulling, still adamantly denying that she pulled. The therapist was patient with her, but Stu and Karen were growing impatient. They wanted to see results quickly and were worried that her friends would start to notice the hair loss and ask questions. In an attempt to motivate Sarah, Karen made statements such as "We are paying a lot of money for this therapy; you need to work harder." Unfortunately, these statements made Sarah feel ashamed, guilty, and confused. She began to shut down and not trust her parents the way she used to, for fear of getting in trouble. Thinking he was being encouraging, Stu commented about her lashes and brows: "You look so much prettier with your eyelashes and eyebrows. Why don't you want them to grow back?" What he did not realize is that she desperately wanted them to grow back.

Sarah began to feel she must be ugly, because her parents kept telling her she was prettier with her lashes and brows, and she had not had them in months. She eventually began to withdraw from friends at school, fearing that they too would judge her harshly for her lack of lashes and brows. Sarah felt misunderstood, blamed, pushed, and frustrated. The common mistake that Stu and Karen made here is called *blaming*.

It is common for parents to feel both frustrated and out of control in response to their child's trich, mainly because it *is* out of parents' control. Moreover, it is difficult for a child to control pulling behavior—but it *is* possible. Parents blame themselves and sometimes inadvertently pass that blame along to their child. But what is a parent to do? Ignoring doesn't work. Pointing out the obvious benefits to having hair doesn't work. What can be done?

It's the Hair Police!

Hannah

Hannah was more than willing to attend sessions with the school counselor each week. Her counselor had purchased a workbook for teens with trich, and she was going through the workbook with Hannah.

Hannah was becoming concerned about her hair loss and was willing to do anything to grow it back. Interestingly, when the counselor gave her homework to do on her own, Hannah was inconsistent. She had some good weeks and some bad weeks with regard to pulling, which was confusing to Hannah, her counselor, and her parents. When her hair started to grow back, her parents praised the hair growth and rewarded her for her success. At other times, however, this "success" was followed immediately by a setback. Peggy and Bob wondered what was wrong with Hannah and why she could not be consistent with the treatment. The more setbacks she had, the more difficult it was to reestablish her motivation.

Soon Hannah began to feel that familiar sense of helplessness and started to give up. Unfortunately, her counselor, who had limited experience with treating trich, also began to feel helpless. She requested fewer visits with Hannah, and eventually they stopped the visits altogether. Hannah began to believe that she would never get control over her pulling and that, as a result, she would never be acceptable to others.

Without intending to do so, Hannah's parents had become the "hair police" and could only see "hair" or "no hair" as a measure of her success. When Hannah came home from school, her parents closely inspected her hair to see if she had pulled any. They thought they were being subtle and that Hannah didn't notice, but she did. She saw the disappointment and sometimes anger in their faces when they noticed that she had pulled. As a result, Hannah began to dread coming home, because she did not want to disappoint them. Good grades on a report card were somehow not as wonderful, because a relapse of hair pulling overshadowed them.

Eventually Hannah began to feel terrible about herself and resentful toward her parents. She felt like they did not understand her and that ultimately they did not care about her as a person. Hannah began to believe that her success with trich was all that mattered. She began to believe that unless she mastered not pulling, she would not be able to live a happy life.

We like to call this mistake *policing*. When parents become so focused on the presence or absence of hair, they literally "police" their child daily about his or her hair status. In addition, parents often feel that they have no other option than to be punitive around hair pulling issues. Some punish their child for pulling or try to get his or her attention by pointing out the hair loss. Others question whether the child really wants to stop.

While it is normal for parents to go through a period of frustration and panic in the beginning, policing can make children feel confused and "down" on themselves. You love your child and want the best for him or her. The last thing you want is to see your child teased or humiliated on the playground for having no eyelashes or a bald spot on his or her head. However, what we have seen clinically is that a punitive approach *does not work*; in fact, it can contribute to feelings of frustration and promote both shame and hopelessness, which exacerbate the problem.

The most powerful feedback children can get is from their peers. However, children younger than eleven often do not care what their hair looks like, so parental or peer feedback usually gets little to no desirable response. When they reach middle school, however, peers may start to tease and make comments. This motivator helps some children become ready to work on their hair pulling.

So what are parents to do? First, you must change your expectations. What makes you proud of your child? Who is he or she, and why is he or she special? It is common for parents to only see "hair or no hair" and inadvertently to dismiss other successes and victories that their child experiences. When you are acting as the hair police, your child learns that hair growth is the most important part of him or her, which can lead to feelings of not measuring up, low self-esteem, and a lack of confidence. You have the power to change this; you have the ability to step out of the role of police and back into the role of supportive parent.

Too Much Focus

Hayden

Hayden also ended up in therapy for trichotillomania. His pulling had been going on for some time and had become so severe that he had developed a large bald spot on his head. Because his therapist had little experience in treating trich, she was alarmed with his level of hair loss. She immediately referred him to a psychiatrist, who put him on antidepressant medication. Most or all of the focus of treatment focused on his pulling. Why was he still pulling despite the medication? Several times the medication was increased and changed. The psychiatrist added other medications to enhance the effect of the antidepressant. Although many side effects emerged, there were no changes in hair pulling.

Ellen took Hayden to his therapy sessions when he was staying with her, and his dad took him when Hayden was at his house. Both parents were defensive about how Hayden did at their respective houses, downplaying the marital discord that had become so prevalent. Even when the therapist tried to turn the focus onto other issues, such as the divorce, they shifted it back to his trich. Hayden continued pulling. Ellen and Fred continued to nag Hayden about his pulling and to pressure him to stop. The mistake that Ellen and Fred make here is called *too much focus* on trich at the expense of other circumstances and on Hayden's qualities and unique attributes.

All four of these common responses—*impatience, blaming, policing, and too much focus*—are widespread among parents. In fact, most well-meaning, good parents have had one, some, or all of these experiences at some point. Although it is important to recognize these reactions in yourself, it is equally important to move forward. Instead of berating yourself for the past, move forward into recognizing and understanding your own feelings, and then learn how you can react differently in the future.

How do you do this? Understanding how you feel is an important first step. In addition, it is helpful to understand hair pulling behavior in a different way—how it is meeting a need for your child. This new perspective on the behavior can help lead to compassion and can alleviate the fear that all parents experience when they discover their child's hair pulling. In the next chapter, we will explore how hair pulling started for each of these four children and how a better understanding of trichotillomania in general helped each parent cope with his or her own fears and reactions.

4

Understanding Leads to Compassion

Trichotillomania as a Soothing Behavior

Ashley

After attending a regional workshop about trichotillomania, Jane obtained some important information about how to understand Ashley. She began to observe Ashley's behavior to try to understand it. Through watching Ashley's hair pulling patterns and talking with her gently about her pulling, Charles and Jane were able to understand that hair pulling was her way of soothing herself to sleep. She cuddled up with her blanket, placed her thumb in her mouth, and started to twirl. The pulling really was more of a side effect of the twirling, rather than a purposeful behavior.

Charles and Jane noticed that pulling happened more frequently when Ashley was overtired or had been particularly busy that day. On days that were less hurried, she pulled less. This information alone helped Charles and Jane with their reactions to Ashley's pulling. First, they realized that her pulling fell into a pattern and as parents, they had some control over the situation. Second, understanding that hair pulling was a soothing behavior helped them to develop compassion for their daughter. Most importantly, they learned *patience* with Ashley. Instead of simply reacting to her hair pulling, Charles and Jane became careful observers of their daughter's behavior.

Jane recalled that when she was tired or overworked during the day, she took a hot bath at night to soothe her and help her settle down. Was this really any different? Charles recalled that as a child he had a soft toy that he rubbed with his fingers (until it literally disintegrated) to help him calm himself. Both Charles and Jane were able to understand Ashley's behavior as adaptive and therefore began to problem solve rather than feel helpless.

Behavior That Begins as Adaptive Can Become a Habit

Sarah

Stu and Karen finally took Sarah to a trained therapist who was able to talk to her about her pulling. Sarah opened up with the therapist because she seemed to know what she was talking about—she seemed to understand her. Sarah reported that she began pulling out her eyelashes several months before, when her allergies had gotten bad in the spring. She had experienced intense itching in her eyes, which led to pulling out her eyelashes to relieve the itching. Soon, the pulling became a habit, especially after the allergies had resolved. After she ran out of eyelashes, pulling moved to her eyebrows as well.

Sarah told the therapist that pulling happened mostly at school, usually during her afternoon classes. She described feeling bored and sometimes confused in school and said that pulling gave her something to do. Sometimes she lined up the hairs on her desk and compared them. Other times she softly rubbed the hair bulb (the plump part at the end of a hair that has been pulled) along her lips because it felt tingly to her and helped her to relax.

Sarah's therapist was able to explain to Stu and Karen how Sarah was using hair pulling as a way of coping. When Sarah was finally able to talk to her parents about her pulling, they were more able to understand her, instead of judge her. Stu and Karen were beginning the process of *accepting* Sarah as having trichotillomania. This did not necessarily mean that they liked it, but that they accepted it is a part of their lives and that it was, in part, how Sarah got her needs met. They were starting to understand their daughter, and the healing was about to begin.

Lifting the Shame

Hannah

Peggy and Bob finally found some answers at a TLC retreat. They took Hannah to a weekend experience where trained professionals were available to help them understand her and learn about her trich. During the weekend, Hannah learned and eventually disclosed that her pulling was complex. She was first drawn to pulling her pubic hair at the onset of puberty. Her pubic hairs were much coarser and thicker than other hair on her body, and she noticed that they had large bulbs attached to them. She began by sitting on the toilet and pulling for thirty to forty-five minutes at a time. It started as a fascination and later turned into a problem.

Feeling mortified to tell her parents that she even had pubic hair, much less that she was pulling it out, she tried to stop on her own. As a result, she moved to pulling her scalp hair. She reasoned that she had much more scalp hair and that she could never pull enough to create a problem. These hairs, she explained, were less coarse and had smaller bulbs, but felt really good to pull. She sat in front of the mirror in the morning and pulled any hairs that were darker, stuck out, or looked out of place. Before long, she could talk herself into pulling any of them. It had become such a part of her morning grooming ritual that she could not imagine stopping.

Hannah said that eventually her hair pulling became more than just a grooming ritual. Over the months, she started to pull when she was worried about peer-related issues. Several girls at school were being mean to her, and pulling had helped her to "think through" the situation and to "feel better." Her pulling was happening during studying and during TV watching, as well as during times of emotional turmoil.

Peggy and Bob were floored. They could not believe how the retreat had helped Hannah be honest about her pulling. The experience of being around other teens had helped her to feel less ashamed about her pulling and more comfortable in her own skin. They noticed that she was acting more like her old self, laughing, smiling, and seemingly happier.

In addition to Hannah changing, Peggy and Bob noticed changes within themselves over the course of the weekend. Peggy noticed that she felt less shame about Hannah's pulling. Talking with other parents who were in the same boat helped Peggy to realize that Hannah's pulling did not make her "weird" or "destined for a life of misery," but was simply something that she did to help her cope in difficult situations. In fact, Peggy was able to talk to several adults who had pulled as children or teens. These people had learned how to manage their pulling and were, much to her delight, normal, lovely adults.

Peggy began to feel more optimistic for Hannah. She felt herself move through her grief and sadness into acceptance and hope. Most importantly, Peggy began to refocus. She began to remember all the wonderful aspects of Hannah: her humor, her independence, her outgoing personality, her compassion for others—things that she had forgotten due to her narrow focus on hair pulling.

Bob had a curative experience through attending the retreat, but in a little different way. He had not experienced shame or fear in response to Hannah's pulling, but he did experience anger. He could not see why she could not quit. Why was it so hard for her to stop? He had taken a black-and-white approach and wanted to punish her for pulling. He witnessed how Hannah's pulling negatively impacted Peggy, and this made him even angrier. More than anything, Bob felt helpless to do anything to help his daughter. He was the man, right? His job was to fix all problems, but why could he not fix this one? Bob felt helpless, ineffective, and impotent.

Through talking with other parents and professionals at the retreat, Bob realized that hair pulling was not under Hannah's control, that stopping was not so simple. He also came to understand that his anger toward Hannah was not helping; in fact, it was hurting her. Bob learned other strategies for coping with his emotions, as well as ways to help Hannah that did not involve blame, punishment, or attempts to control her behavior. He learned how to avoid power struggles with his daughter and how to engage her in productive, fruitful conversation. As a result, Bob felt less helpless and more hopeful about the future.

Hair Pulling in Context

Hayden

Hayden stopped seeing the psychiatrist and was eventually taken off all medications. After finding a behavior therapy group in their area with a trained therapist who had much experience in treating individuals with trich, Ellen and Fred began to get answers. They learned that medications were not the first line of intervention for trich and no medication consistently worked for reducing hair pulling symptoms. The new therapist was able to explain that Hayden's trich may or may not have had anything to do with his parents' divorce, but it had become the focus of much of the parental discord and a way for him to deal with unpleasant feelings.

Through family therapy, Ellen and Fred learned that Hayden pulled to relieve stress and to soothe himself in a variety of emotionally difficult situations. Academic pressure, boredom, and intense sensory experiences while playing with the hair all perpetuated his pulling. He was soothing himself on many different levels: physical (sensory), emotional, and psychological.

Once the therapy began to broaden to family-based issues and Ellen and Fred learned appropriate communication skills with each other, as well as with their children, things started to improve. Through treatment with the entire family, the therapist was able to identify a multitude of coping strategies that each of their children had adopted to deal with their new family situation. By looking at trich in the context of the larger family system, Ellen and Fred were able to have compassion for all their children and to learn more appropriate ways of intervening and communicating with each one.

As these case studies have demonstrated, different parental reactions to a child's pulling can have a negative effect on the hair pulling and on the family dynamics. It is both natural and common to have a big, sometimes negative initial reaction when you discover that your child is pulling out hair. However, through understanding your child's unique situation, you will likely develop compassion for your child, and ultimately you will be ready to intervene in a proactive and helpful manner. In the next chapter, we will look at what you can do to assist your child in his or her journey to recovery.

5

OK, What Do I Do Now?

Address Readiness Issues

What strategies should you use for success? A reasonable question but difficult to answer. The most important thing is, are you ready to take the next step in helping your child? Regardless of whether you are the parent of a very young child, an elementary school-aged child, or a child in middle school or high school, you will need time, energy, and support to be successful. As is true with any childhood problem, the parents are always somewhat involved in the process of managing the issue. Sometimes the involvement is all encompassing, as with very young children. At other times, parents are involved in the organization and oversight. Most of the time, the parents are lead cheerleaders, major support systems, and troubleshooters. Just thinking about it can be overwhelming.

There are some important questions you should ask yourself: Given all of the important roles you play, do you have the time and energy to devote to this cause? Is this the right time for your family? Is this the right time for you? If so, it is just as important for you to commit to this process as it is for your child. Many times, parents have trouble staying consistent with the strategies suggested and end up dropping the ball for very good reasons. Parents have numerous responsibilities, family obligations, children's activities, and work-related tasks to tend to daily. It's important to take all of this into consideration when deciding if this is the right time to start working on hair pulling.

Take care of yourself. Do you have the emotional resources necessary to embark on this process? If not, what do you need? How can you get support? Make sure that you have some recreational time for yourself. Develop some good hobbies that are stress relieving: reading, exercise, time with friends, sports, card games, or whatever you might enjoy. In sum, first make sure you are ready and able to make a commitment to helping your child in a calm and responsible fashion, and second, take steps to care for yourself along the way. This is a wonderful opportunity to become a role model for your child about how to approach a difficult problem with acceptance and grace.

We want our children to be able take a step back, gather the resources necessary to address their problems, and garner support to be successful. As parents, we need to do this first. Demonstrate for your child how it is done. Recognize your needs, and try to meet those needs to best of your ability. Modeling can be an important tool to help your child—and in the process, yourself.

In addition to evaluating your own readiness to embark on this journey, also make sure that the family is prepared. It may mean that there is more time and energy devoted to one child. If your family is already experiencing stress (due to marital difficulties, another child with robust issues in need of attention, or communication difficulties frequently leading to arguments), you will need to attend to these issues first. Although these family dynamics may not have caused the hair pulling, they will undoubtedly contribute to it at some point. It is normal for families to experience stress (moving to a new area, a death in the family, divorce, and so on) and challenges. In response to stress, families must develop good coping skills to function well.

If your family is experiencing acute challenges, you may want to address these first, before devoting yourselves to working on hair pulling. Changing behavior can be a time-consuming task that requires focus and energy. By addressing pressing or acute matters first, your family may be more ready and better equipped to handle the challenges that trichotillomania may present.

Be Patient: Take a Deep Breath and Slow Down

Ashley

As they watched Ashley's patterns and learned about her pulling behavior, Charles and Jane decided to take a step back and do some research about trichotillomania in very young children, or what has been referred to as "baby trich." This process took patience. Each day, Charles and Jane read a website or article. At the end of the day, they shared with each other what they had learned. After a few weeks, they were more informed about trichotillomania in general and about baby trich specifically. Just reading about other families dealing with similar problems helped them feel validated and hopeful. They began to believe that their situation could improve.

Charles and Jane decided to talk with someone who had treated a number of children with preschool hair pulling, even though that professional did not live in their state. They had several hour-long phone consultations with this therapist to learn what she knew and to tell her what they had observed in Ashley. The therapist remarked at how wonderfully they were doing with observing and watching—and being *patient*. She told Jane that patience with Ashley would eventually lead Ashley to feel calm, safe, and nurtured. Gathering information from a very knowledgeable source made them feel much better.

Jane understood that the strategies would be mostly her responsibility and that she needed to be emotionally prepared. She decided to take a yoga class with a friend. This gave her some much-needed time to herself doing something that she loved and provided her with good exercise three times a week. Jane also decided to join a mom's group. This allowed her some adult interaction, and Ashley had some other kids to play with. Even though the other moms were not coping with their children pulling hair, they were all struggling in one way or another with behavioral issues and how to parent. This made

Jane feel more like a "normal" parent, and she was able to open up and confide with these women about her struggle with Ashley's pulling.

Jane realized that gathering information, finding time for herself, and developing a support system all helped prepare her to work on Ashley's pulling. Being *patient* with herself made a huge difference in Jane's outlook. It also helped her become more patient with Ashley. Things would not change overnight, or even in a week, but Jane was feeling better in general and could see that, given time and patience, change would occur.

Do you find yourself becoming impatient with your child? Have you ever snapped at him or her for pulling or even fiddling with hair? If so, try to exercise *patience* with your child. Take deep breaths, walk away, take a break, or make a neutral statement or no statement at all when you want to snap.

Move Toward Acceptance

Sarah

Stu and Karen decided to speak with someone who knew about trichotillomania. They gathered reading material and talked about their feelings. Karen realized Sarah's appearance embarrassed her. In addition, Karen felt that she had failed her daughter as a mother and blamed herself for Sarah's pulling. These feelings of blame and embarrassment deeply affected how Karen felt about herself as a mother, not to mention how she felt about Sarah. Karen realized that she also blamed Sarah for making her feel terrible.

Once Karen understood her feelings, it was easier (not easy, though) to examine them. Over time, Karen began to *accept* that she was not to blame for Sarah's pulling and that Sarah would work on hair pulling when she was ready. She learned that *accepting* Sarah's hair pulling did not mean that she condoned it or that she was resigning herself to "allow" it to continue. It simply meant that hair pulling was a part of how Sarah copes, for now.

If Karen could help, she would be happy to, but Sarah needed to be willing to work on managing her pulling on her own. It would never have occurred to Karen that she might need some help when dealing with Sarah's hair pulling, but once she accepted that it was neither her fault nor Sarah's, it became much less tense around the house.

Sarah soon started talking to her parents again like she used to, because her parents had stopped saying negative things about her hair. An important breakthrough happened one day when Sarah came home from school after a particularly boring math class where she'd pulled out all of her eyelashes again. When she got home, she braced herself for the inspection and the usual "guilt trip"—except it didn't happen. Karen sat down and asked Sarah about her day. She listened as Sarah complained about math. Then she got up from her seat and prepared a special snack for Sarah, because she'd had a tough math class. Nothing was said about Sarah's hair, the money they were spending on therapy, or whether Sarah was ready to stop pulling. Sarah was so relieved that she almost cried. This allowed her to open up slowly and helped Karen to feel closer to her. Their relationship improved, and they become more of a team rather than behaving as if they were opponents.

Sarah began to *accept* herself. Karen began to *accept* Sarah. And the whole family *accepted* that trichotillomania was part of the family—for the moment. It didn't mean that anyone was a bad child or a bad parent, just that this was what was happening in the family for the time being. Have you accepted trich as a part of your child's life and you family's life? Do you find yourself just wishing that it would go away? Remember, *accepting* does not mean condoning hair pulling, or even liking it; it means simply acknowledging that it *is* in your life.

Release, Don't Police

Hannah

Peggy and Bob were exhausted with being the hair police. They hated doing it, and Hannah hated it even more. The TLC weekend retreat helped Peggy to understand Hannah and why she was pulling and to have compassion for her as a developing adolescent. Adolescence is hard enough. Peggy started to talk to Hannah about her feelings, not her hair. At the retreat, Peggy learned that she wasn't helping by policing and that she needed to stop. This was very hard for her. She started talking to Bob for support and made a plan to *release*, not police.

Peggy took deep breaths every time she wanted to comment on hair or to tell Hannah to "get your hand out of your hair." The breathing helped Peggy to relax a bit. She made a point of not saying anything about hair for one day. Then she added another day to her goal and so on. Soon Peggy was able to go for long periods without saying anything about Hannah's hair, and her deep breathing allowed her to *release* tension around hair pulling issues. Eventually, Peggy noticed that as she was changing, and so was Hannah. Hannah began to relax.

Although Hannah continued to pull her hair, she and Peggy began to talk about a variety of things, like other mothers and daughters. Once Hannah felt more comfortable, she and Peggy started to talk about the hair pulling in a different way. Peggy asked Hannah if there was anything she could do to help. Hannah was surprised and delighted by her mother's view of her as the expert. Hannah suggested a system to help her remember to use her strategies. Rather than nagging, Hannah came up with a secret word that Peggy was to use when Hannah was pulling or had her hand in her hair. This code word made Hannah laugh, so when she heard her mother say it, she was able to use her strategies right away.

Peggy realized what a difference it made to be able to *release* and not police. Her relationship improved with her daughter, and Peggy felt much better about herself. Do you find yourself policing your child and his or her hair? Do you catch yourself inspecting hair growth, nagging when you see hair play, or responding negatively to obvious pulling? If so, try to police yourself. Make a commitment to let go of or *release* your desire to control your child; the results may surprise you.

Change Your Focus

Hayden

Through intensive family therapy and individual treatment for trich, Hayden stopped pulling. He turned his energy toward sports and became involved in basketball. His father played basketball in high school as well, so it allowed them to spend time together practicing and talking. Their relationship healed, and Hayden stopped blaming his father for leaving the family.

Ellen and Fred learned that the most important people in their lives were their children, and together they decided to put them first. They learned not to blame each other when things went wrong and stopped putting the children in the middle of their relationship. Most importantly, they learned to *focus* on Hayden's accomplishments, not his struggles—especially not his trich. All too often parents become too focused on hair and hair pulling issues, much to the detriment of their child's development and self-esteem. The outcome of this shift in *focus* was that Hayden improved dramatically in basketball and was recognized as an outstanding player by the school. His self-esteem grew and the need to soothe himself through hair pulling decreased.

Where is your focus with regard to your child? Do you tend to focus too much on issues surrounding hair? Have you neglected important aspects of your child that need attention? If so, shift your *focus* to these other areas, and see what happens as a result.

Although, in these examples, each child is pulling his or her hair, every child has a distinct experience. In addition, parents and professionals should deal with hair pulling somewhat differently, depending on the child's age and stage of development. In the next chapter, we will explore trichotillomania from infancy through high school, addressing the differing therapeutic needs at each developmental stage.

6

Different Ages and Different Stages of Trich

Baby Trich

Trichotillomania looks different during different ages and developmental stages. It is important to understand your child's developmental stage in order to understand his or her hair pulling adequately. For example, some people believe that hair pulling under the age of five is not trichotillomania exactly, but rather a phenomenon known as baby trich. With baby trich, children do not always develop full-blown trichotillomania when they get older and may even outgrow it. A common recommendation at this age is to ignore the behavior and let it go away on its own. What if it doesn't go away? What if you can't ignore it?

We have learned that early intervention can be enormously successful and that children who have learned to manage hair pulling at an early age are not likely to develop it later. This suggests that the "wait and see if she grows out of it" approach is not always advisable.

So, what does hair pulling look like for the very young? Very young children who engage in hair pulling often combine it with other self-soothing behaviors. For these youngsters, hair pulling usually occurs when the child is sucking his or her thumb or fingers. In addition, most children pull when they are tired or slightly bored. These times usually include lying down for a nap, riding in the car, going to sleep for the night, or waking up. Other times might include listening to a story or watching TV. Some children at this age do not suck their thumbs or fingers, but do pull their hair. However, for these kids, the situations usually mirror those of children who suck their thumbs.

Children at this age are learning new things every minute of every day. This is a wonderful time to introduce how to be tired or cranky without pulling hair. Also, it's an excellent opportunity to introduce alternate self-soothing techniques. Most children at this age are very interested in exploring their world. But they are limited in how they explore it. Children use their senses to discover things at this age. Therefore, examining the texture of something, how something feels in the mouth or rubbed on the face or head, is very important. It is also an opportunity to soothe themselves, because these different things feel good. Remember, what feels good to a baby or toddler does not always feel good to an adult. Also, what feels good to one person may not feel good to someone else. Don't assume that because hair pulling hurts to you that it also hurts to your child. Very often this behavior feels good, is comforting, and provides some interest for your child.

If your young child is pulling hair, you may be wondering, *How does this apply to me and my child? What am I supposed to do?* First, you need to observe when your child is likely to engage in hair pulling. As mentioned earlier, usually these times include, but are not limited to, when your child is tired, going to sleep, or waking up; listening to a story or book; watching TV or a video; and in the car. If your child sucks his or her thumb, as Ashley does, this can contribute to or trigger hair pulling as well.

For all children, sensory stimulation is important. But unlike older children, little children do not have the cognitive capability to work on modifying their own behavior. Therefore, blocking the ability to pull is an important first step. Have your child wear a very pretty, lightweight pair of gloves during times when he or she is more likely to pull. These gloves usually can be found around Easter or are in wedding shops. Other possibilities are gloves with finger puppets or sock puppets. Your child can wear the gloves at night and receive a sticker or small reward in the morning for waking up with the gloves on. It's important to use fun, appealing, and lightweight gloves or sock puppets. Children usually dislike wearing winter gloves, because they are hot and cumbersome. They are less likely to reject comfortable, appealing gloves. In addition, giving a little reward for compliance can help your child feel good about the process.

Sensory input is also important. And children need to have lots of it. Having you or your child brush his or her hair can feel good.

(Children should not run their hands through their hair, however. It's too tempting.) Introduce interesting brushes or combs to your child to see what he or she prefers. Also provide highly tactile toys such as latch-hook rugs, yarn, or textured balls in trigger situations to allow your child to address tactile needs. Just like with any behavior at this age, you are shaping your child's new behavior by encouraging alternative activities.

Remember that rewards will be very helpful at this stage. Stickers or little grab-bag toys are highly appealing and keep the child interested in the behavior change. Nothing is more rewarding, however, than Mommy and/or Daddy clapping, smiling, and hugging them. All rewards should be given with this type of enthusiasm. Remember that you are rewarding the use of strategies (wearing gloves, using tactile toys, playing with finger puppets), not hair growth.

This type of program is often very hard to do on your own. It usually requires support and regular adjustments to be successful. Working with a therapist who specializes in treating young children might be very helpful. If this is not possible, working with an occupational therapist who has experience with small children may be a good alternative.

To help a young child with hair pulling, we must understand his or her hair pulling behavior: what need it is addressing, when the behavior is most likely to occur, and what sensations the child is gaining from the behavior. As you may recall, Jane noticed that Ashley pulled more on days that were long or when she was overtired. This information gave Jane and her husband some idea of how to change situations to make them less high risk. They decided to limit activities during the day to keep Ashley from becoming overtired, provided light gloves for her at night, and made sure that she had plenty of soothing downtime in the evening to wind down.

During treatment, your therapist will develop a behavioral plan and will provide strategies to help your child practice alternate ways to cope with emotional and sensory experiences. This is a delicate process. Your therapist should help you to make this process fun. Otherwise, situations can deteriorate quickly into a battle of wills, which you will always lose. Therefore, it is useful that you have, as mentioned before, the energy, enthusiasm, and support to be able to work on the behavior.

It is equally important to know your child's temperament and stage of development to ensure a successful experience. Very young children vary widely in their development. Some children are pre-verbal, and others are talking up a storm. Some children are headstrong and want to do everything themselves, while others are agreeable and compliant. It's important to know what stage he or she is in. If your child is in the "no" stage, you may want to wait a few months to start introducing strategies to help with hair pulling. If your child is just beginning potty training, now may not be a good time to introduce yet another way to control your child's behavior.

The good news is, children go through these stages quickly. If you wait a few weeks, or sometimes a month or two, your child will be on to other things. It's never going to be ideal, but there are some stages, such as potty training, moving, or introducing a new sibling that are more difficult than others.

The Elementary School Child

For children under the age of twelve, trichotillomania affects as many boys as it does girls. After the age of twelve, girls outnumber boys with trich nine to one. As far as we know, there have not been any long-term studies on children with baby trich to determine if these children do indeed "grow out of" trich or if they do develop it later in life. The usual course of the disorder is that it waxes and wanes over many years before taking solid hold. Younger children often are very confused about their pulling. They experience such pleasure with pulling, yet they sense their parents' unhappiness with the behavior.

Children younger than twelve typically are less concerned with hair loss than those who have reached middle school with all its peer pressures. As a result, treatment may consist of providing rewards to encourage the use of strategies. Children this young may not work for hair growth, but often they will work for a reward.

Children at this stage (five to twelve years) need more than anything to feel loved and accepted. Anxiety is common in children in the elementary school years, and feeling unaccepted, punished, shamed, or humiliated can lead to fear, confusion, insecurity, and anxiety. If your child is in these middle years, make it very clear that your love and acceptance is unconditional. This means that whether or not your child is pulling out hair, completely bald, or lacking eyelashes or eyebrows, he or she is a valued, loved, and cherished individual.

Many times you may need to bite your tongue when you want to comment or "help." However, it's good to educate your child about trich; let him or her know that hair pulling is just a small part of who he or she is, and that you love the whole package. Help yourself begin to accept trich as a way of coping with difficult situations. Make sure you (or a therapist) are teaching your child alternate coping strategies for these situations.

Acceptance requires you to work on your feelings of frustration and shame. You must get your feelings in check before you can expect your child to do the same. Children absolutely need to feel like their parents are in control and can handle all kinds of situations. When children suspect that their parents feel out of control or, worse, that they are in control of how their parents feel, they may become frightened. If your reactions to your child resemble crying, begging, terror, rage, blaming, hysteria, or other intense emotional turmoil, your child is likely in control. If your reaction is empathy—"I am sorry you had a hard day. Do you want to talk about it?"—instead of "I can't believe how much you pulled!" or "This is horrible! People are going to think you are weird, and you won't have any friends," your child will feel safe and will believe that you can handle yourself and the situation.

If anxiety is present during this time in the form of fears, phobias, obsessions, compulsions, or avoidance, be careful not to attribute this solely to trich. It is common for children to have some anxiety during the elementary years. Children at this age need to feel safe within the structure of the home and require clear expectations and consequences. Loose structure or vague expectations within the family can lead children to feel anxious and sometimes to act out. The resultant anxiety is completely separate from trich. Two common mistakes that parents make in reaction to trich are further loosening the home structure or becoming overly strict yet unpredictable with regard to expectations and consequences. These approaches only make matters worse and more confusing for the child and can lead to more insecurity and anxiety—and more pulling.

In the late-elementary and middle school years, children are fragile with regard to self-esteem. Help your budding adolescent feel pride and accomplishment for things that he or she is good at doing. Try not to focus on hair pulling, but rather focus on sports, art, academics, theater, writing, hobbies, and so on. If your child has not yet found a particular area of strength, provide opportunities for him or her to experience a variety of new activities. Be supportive of different ideas, and praise your child for trying new things, even if they are a struggle.

The Middle School Child

Middle school is a time of tremendous change for children, both physically and emotionally. In treatment, the types of strategies selected and the level of parent involvement depend largely on the child's temperament, maturity, and relationship with the parent. Some early adolescents are happy to have their parents involved in helping them. Others feel the need for greater independence from their parents. With the help of a therapist, determine how much involvement is going to be helpful to your child, as well as when to back off. Trained professionals assist children in talking about feelings and can help parents feel more comfortable taking less of a leadership role.

Middle school is typically the time when children begin to experience teasing from their peers because of their hair pulling and for other reasons. Your role is to support your child, so that he or she is able to cope with these unfortunate interactions. Instead of using teasing as a way for you to make your point about why he or she should stop pulling, give your child the words to cope with these encounters. For example, Peggy and Bob taught Hannah to how to respond to peers who asked her, "What happened to your hair?" with "I have trichotillomania. Go look it up!" Hannah reported that other kids were so confused that they just walked away and eventually left her alone. She thought it was funny that she knew a word that other kids did not know, much less how to spell. Middle school is hard enough on kids, but having trich can make it seem almost unbearable. It is helpful to find ways to make having trich more tolerable for your child.

Sometimes parents need to intervene at the school to educate the faculty and administration about hair pulling or to make school personnel aware of brutality that may be going on toward their child. You can get educational literature to address school-related issues from the TLC. Often we recommend that a child wear a hat at school, if this is a common pulling place for him or her. Because most schools prohibit the wearing of hats, consult your school administration and get permission for this. In addition, if pulling occurs in class, the use of a hand strategy such as a puzzle eraser, ticky tack, or a small koosh ball may help. Get the permission and understanding of the teacher to avoid potential confusion, such as the teacher thinking your child is messing around in class. In any event, your middle school child may need the extra assistance of a therapist to negotiate this difficult period. Provide this opportunity if your child is receptive, and keep your focus on what is truly important: your child's self-esteem.

The High School Child

High school years bring unique challenges. Teenagers can be defiant and angry just by nature—when you add trich to the picture, whew! A great challenge that parents of adolescents face is managing their children's unpleasant behaviors without damaging the relationship. First, you need to understand that the struggle for independence in adolescence (the back talk, the eye rolls, the pushing of limits) is a normal part of the individuation process—the process by which adolescents become increasingly independent from their parents in an attempt to discover who they are as separate people from their parents. Adolescents do this in a variety of ways, such as changing hair color, disregarding rules, slacking off on academics, becoming sexually active, or experimenting with alcohol and drugs. While this limit testing is somewhat normal, it is your responsibility to be aware of and involved in your adolescent's activities—that is, know what your child is up to and set appropriate expectations and consequences. As if this isn't enough, adding trich to the equation can really create a mess.

The most common mistake we see parents of adolescents make is allowing hair pulling to become a point of contention with their children. If your child knows that hair pulling will absolutely send you over the edge, guess what he or she is going to do when mad at you? Adolescents know exactly what is going to punish you, and they are likely going to do it. Sometimes parents avoid doling out punishment for misbehavior, because they are afraid it will lead to increased pulling. This is very dangerous, as it allows the adolescent to be in control and not suffer necessary consequences to poor behavior. Do not allow the fear of hair pulling to prevent you from giving appropriate and deserved consequences.

If trich has become a way for your child to "get back at you," this can change, but it will take effort on your part. First you must stop reacting to the hair pulling, no matter how obvious and extreme it is. Your lack of reaction lets your child know that the pulling only hurts him or her, not you. Eventually, your child will turn to other strategies for "winning" the battle against you.

Hair pulling is unique at each age and stage of development, and so is parenting. Your role as a parent changes as your child does, and so does your role as an advocate to help your child manage hair pulling. Being a good advocate requires a delicate balance of support, compassion, and knowledge. In the next chapter, we will look at what you need to know when considering treatment.

7

The Nuts and Bolts of Treatment

What to Know

What is important to know about treatment for trich? Is it all the same? Are some treatments better than others? As scientists, we know that we must look to research to see what types of interventions have been proven to work with real people in the real world. The interventions that have been effective in scientific studies are those that involve behavioral analysis (understanding the behavior), teaching specific coping strategies, and a long-term commitment to and management of behavioral change.

Before we describe the behavioral treatment for trich, it is important to talk about medications. Parents frequently ask about medicine because some want a magic bullet to cure their child, while others have been steered in that direction by a medical professional and are concerned about medicating. Scientific investigations show that no medication works well for everyone, and no medication has received approval from the FDA for the treatment of trich. Several studies indicate improvement with medications for some people, but often the improvement is short lived. As trich is a waxing and waning condition, it is hard to tell if the improvement is a placebo effect (a result of the child expecting to get better with the medication), if it is a function of the natural ups and downs of trich, or if the medication is truly responsible.

Frequently, kids who are depressed or anxious and who pull when they are having these feelings may benefit from taking antidepressant medications. Sometimes the trich is helped when other symptoms improve. If no other symptoms are present (like depression or anxiety), it is uncertain whether antidepressant medication is helpful in reducing urges to pull hair.

Currently, in early 2013, there have been no medication studies concerning children with trichotillomania. The studies with adults have had minimal results, so there are no drug-use guidelines for trichotillomania. All medication use for children who pull is "off-label" treatment, which means that the medication is prescribed for a use the FDA has not approved. Conversations with your child's psychiatrist will help you to make an informed decision.

It is common for children with trichotillomania to have ADHD also. Attention problems are important to treat, because attention and concentration affect educational development and career success, as well as confidence, self-esteem, and self-image. A frequent question from parents of kids with ADHD is "Will the medication make my child's trich worse?" The answer is not straight-forward. Although some children do seem to pull more on stimulant medication (and some actually begin pulling when stimulant medication is introduced), this is not always the case. Clinically, we see that some children do better with their pulling while on stimulant medication, so we cannot predict how a child will react.

When stimulants do make pulling more pronounced, it is important to consider several things before making a decision. First, untreated attention problems can cause lifelong issues for your child if education is affected. Children who are not able to pay attention in class miss valuable instruction and can miss out on important foundational learning, which affects future educational opportunities and ultimately may reduce self-esteem.

So what is a parent to do? Consult with a psychiatrist who has some training in trich and ADHD. You may have to go out of your immediate area to get a consultation, but it is worth it. There are types of medications not in the stimulant class that also treat attention issues. Sometimes these are a better choice than traditional ADHD medications. When stimulant medications are the only choice, really beefing up the behavioral therapy to compensate for increased urges and automatic pulling is recommended.

There is preliminary evidence that a supplement, N-Acetyl Cysteine (NAC) may be helpful in the treatment of trichotillomania. NAC is an amino acid that works in the glutamate system of the brain.

We know that the glutamate system helps with the feeling of pleasure. A study conducted by Jon Grant in 2009 showed that 56 percent of subjects with trichotillomania significantly reduced their hair pulling when taking NAC. One explanation may be that increasing the feeling of pleasure in the brain leads to less seeking of pleasure through pulling. Patients who have experienced success using NAC report: "I just don't think about pulling anymore; it does not feel as good to me." Interestingly, only about half of people respond to this supplement. A recent study conducted by Dr. Michael Bloch showed a poor response to NAC in children with trich. We are not sure why some people respond to NAC and some do not, particularly with regard to children. Talk to your pediatrician or psychiatrist and ask them to read the 2009 article about NAC and trich. He or she should be able to guide you as to whether or not to try this supplement with your child and, if so, about appropriate dosages.

What we do know is that behavioral treatment conducted with a motivated child and a willing family *is* successful. We see children and adolescents reduce and stop pulling their hair all the time. However, much like a diet and exercise program, behavioral treatment takes time, effort, and energy.

We have already talked a lot about how best to parent a child with trich. In behavioral treatment, a good therapist will work with you, as parents, to avoid *impatience*, *blaming*, *policing*, and *too much focus* on hair. The key to parenting a child with trich is simple: accept and love your child as he or she is. A therapist working with your child will also add the following essential components:

1. Assess all sensory, cognitive, affective, motor, and situational components of your child's hair pulling, after which a functional analysis or behavioral analysis is designed.
2. Tailor the intervention by choosing specific coping strategies based on the information from the analysis.
3. Evaluate what interventions work with your child.
4. Develop a plan for long-term maintenance of treatment gains and relapse prevention.

The first several sessions of treatment are spent not only educating parents and helping them to be less reactive, but also focusing on helping the child to be more aware of his or her behavior. Back in chapter one, we talked about the five components that contributed to a child's pulling behavior. This next section will flesh out what those components are and why we pay such close attention to them.

Sensory Aspects of Pulling

Although trich is different for each individual, people report some common experiences. The first area evaluated in therapy is the sensory component of pulling. All of the senses can be involved in the pulling process (touch, sight, taste, smell, and hearing).

Let's look at touch. Many people report pulling because of sensations in the fingers before, during, or because of pulling. For example, it is common for children to enjoy the way that pulling the hair through their fingers feels. Sometimes they isolate hairs with certain textures (coarse, thick, wiry, curly, thin, bumpy) that give the tips of the fingers a particular sensation. It is common for people to stroke their hair prior to pulling or to run the hair through their fingers after pulling it out. All of these behaviors address the sense of touch. Over the years, we have noticed that people who pull have amazing tactile sensitivity. They are able to feel subtle differences between hairs and to differentiate between hairs that are "good" to pull and those that "should be left alone." Touch can also be experienced on the skin (at the site of pulling). For some, the sensation that occurs as they remove the hair is the most pleasurable.

The second sensation that we look at is visual. Sometimes children search visually for hair with certain qualities, such as color (darker or lighter), texture (coarser, thicker, or bumpier), or some other aspect of the hair that is unusual (hairs that stick out, are curly or straightened, have split ends, or look different in another way). With regard to eyelashes and eyebrows, visual triggers are common. Sometimes mirrors are used to identify hairs that are irregular, making bathrooms high-risk places.

For many people with trich, the visual aspects of pulling occur after they pull it out. They frequently examine and analyze hair or the bulb at the tip of the hair. Many people report pulling hairs that they believe will have a large bulb. It is common for children to play with the hair or the bulb. Many people pull off the bulb or rub the bulb along their face or mouth (a touch sensation).

The sensations of taste, smell, and hearing are less common. About 13 percent of people report that they bite or eat the bulb and/or the whole hair (a taste sensation). Eating hair in large quantities can be dangerous to the digestive tract; consequently, a good therapist will always ask about hair ingestion. If your child is eating the hair, it is important to have him or her evaluated by a gastroenterologist for the possibility of a trichobezoar (hair ball) in the gut. These are rare, but can be life threatening.

Sometimes hair has an interesting odor, so the child smells it either before or after pulling it. For some youngsters, the sound of the hair being pulled out or the bulb being "popped" in the mouth is motivating. Some report that when they pull out an eyelash, the eyelid "slaps" back against the eyeball, making a popping noise. All of these sensory experiences are important to evaluate. Once evaluated, the therapist will select specific coping strategies that will either help the child satisfy his or her sensory needs in a manner other than pulling or will decrease the availability of the sensory stimulus, thus decreasing the sensory trigger that leads to pulling.

Another aspect of the sensory modality is how all sensory information is integrated into a child's brain. We are all constantly taking in sensory information: smells, noises, touch sensations, visual information, and so on. Some children have difficulty integrating all this information and can become overwhelmed. Kids who are prone to sensory difficulties (those who don't like tags, loud noises, bright lights, textures) may be more prone to trich. Although there is currently no research looking at sensory integration and trichotillomania, we see clinically that hair pulling behavior may be a way for children to help all the sensory information to integrate into the brain. So, for example, when a child is sitting in class, listening to a teacher, looking at a multitude of pictures and maps on the walls, listening to little Suzie next to her make noises, and feeling her itchy sweater that she did not want to wear, she may pull her hair to help her to integrate all this information. In this scenario, pulling seems to calm down the nervous systems when on overload.

With another student in the same situation, his nervous system may feel under-stimulated due to sitting still and listening to a teacher give lots of information. In this case, he may feel bored and pulling might energize his under-stimulated nervous system. So the same situation could result in pulling for the opposite reason. Therefore, it is extremely important for the therapist and child to understand pulling behavior in order to choose and implement the best strategies for each situation.

Thoughts Are Important Too

Sometimes children develop beliefs or automatic thoughts that can lead to pulling. Thoughts may be permission giving, such as "I will just pull this one" or "I deserve this," or they can be mistaken beliefs about hair pulling, such as "I can't focus without pulling" or "I have to get all the split ends out or I will look bad." Evaluating these thoughts and beliefs can lead to simple and effective interventions.

Thoughts can also be perfectionistic, such as "All my eyelashes must be pointing the same way" or "This eyebrow must match the other exactly." Recognizing and understanding maladaptive thoughts or faulty beliefs can lead to specific, helpful strategies for behavior change; this constitutes the *cognitive* in the cognitive behavioral model of therapy.

How Feelings Play a Part

As discussed in chapter one, the American Psychiatric Association's 1994 manual says a diagnosis of trichotillomania requires that a person experience tension prior to pulling and gratification or relief during the pulling. However, studies have demonstrated that many other feelings precede pulling, and a host of other emotions are experienced during and after an episode. Dr. Gretchen Deifenbach and her colleagues found that some people with trich pull when they are experiencing boredom, sadness, worry, or frustration. In addition, people report positive feelings during pulling, such as relaxation, happiness, calmness, or even increased energy or concentration.

Unfortunately, hair pulling can result in feelings of frustration, anger, guilt, and shame, which can leave a child at risk for another episode. In other words, "it feels good" may be an accurate statement, but the good feeling is short lived and is usually followed by feeling bad. Helping a child to recognize, understand, and manage his or her emotional states can be essential in helping him or her to combat trich.

Busy Hands

Many children with trich have a higher than normal need to fiddle or play with things in their hands. These kids always have something in hand—and sometimes it is hair. If this is the case, they can employ strategies to keep their hands busy, to avoid putting them in their hair. Strategies are particularly useful if a therapist tailors them to meet any "touch" preferences that are present. For example, play dough, pipe cleaners, koosh balls, and bubble wrap are all useful "hand toys" that not only keep a child's hands busy, but also provide interesting textures and sensations on the fingers and hands. As we will see, one key to successful management of hair pulling is to focus on, encourage, and reward alternative behaviors, rather than focusing on the hair or the pulling itself.

It is important to evaluate this "motor" behavior and understand how aware the child is of his or her pulling at a given time. For many children, at least some of the pulling occurs completely outside of their awareness. This is referred to as "automatic" pulling. During these trigger situations, the child might be watching TV, reading, riding in the car, or sitting in class, completely unaware of what his or her hands are up to. For these types of pulling episodes, it is very important to spend time in treatment on awareness training. It is nearly impossible to change a behavior if we are not even aware that we are doing it.

Environmental Triggers and Acquired Habits

Although current theories explain that hair pulling is more complex than simply a habit, there is still a habitual component to the behavior for many children. Hair pulling tends to occur in certain predictable situations. Situations can be a time of day, a place, or an activity. Most children can name two or three central places or activities in which they tend to pull. Common hair pulling places may include the bedroom, bathroom, car, classroom, or den.

Common activities include, but are not limited to, trying to fall asleep, working on the computer, getting ready for bed, sitting on the toilet, sitting in the backseat of the car on a long trip, listening to a boring or confusing lecture in school, reading, studying, talking on the phone, or watching TV. Sometimes children pull only when they are alone, which can be a trigger in and of itself. Some pull in front of other people, but are discreet about how they do it. Some children are triggered to pull by seeing common, household objects such as tweezers or mirrors. Hair pulling often takes place during sedentary activities. Knowing where and when hair pulling takes place is wonderful information so that coping strategies can be used in these high-risk situations.

It Just Feels Good

Whereas most of us would say that pulling hair hurts, people with trich report some physical sensations that are pleasant or interesting, or that relieve discomfort. In reality, why would anyone pull if it hurt? The truth is, to those with trich, some aspect of the pulling behavior feels very good. Some children report physical pleasure with pulling, such as tingling or soothing sensations on the skin. Other young people describe itching, burning, or discomfort on the skin prior to pulling that is somehow relieved by the removal of hair. Still others report that the actual pulling of hair is uncomfortable but the sensory stimulation and exploration of the hair after the pull is extremely satisfying. The relief of the bad sensation or achieving an extremely satisfying good sensation is, therefore, very reinforcing. In either case, hair pulling provides very real relief or satisfaction to the puller. The "feels good" sensation can be physical, visual, cognitive, emotional, or neurological. It is the job of the therapist, with the help of the child, to unravel the complex behavior of hair pulling and to identify strategies for change.

Completing the Assessment

To complicate matters, most children report many combinations of all of these sensory, cognitive, motor, emotional, and situational factors. These combinations require a complex and individualized approach to treatment. For example, a child may sometimes pull when getting ready for bed (in the bathroom, tired, looking in the mirror, and visually looking for hairs of a certain type). That same child might also pull when in class (bored, hand near the head, feeling for coarse hairs). These two high-risk situations require completely different interventions. Once the assessment is complete, appropriate strategies such as behavioral substitutes, sensory distractions, coping techniques, relaxation strategies, and cognitive restructuring may be selected to help the child in his or her high-risk situations.

Evaluation and Positive Reinforcement

After a variety of interventions are tried over several weeks, the therapist, child, and (sometimes) the parent evaluate what is working and what is not working for the child. The therapist makes adjustments and modifications as needed. The therapist identifies key strategies along the way, and the child is positively reinforced for using those strategies.

It is very important to remember that the focus should be on the use of strategies, not on hair growth. If a child is using strategies, the hair pulling behavior will decrease, and the hair will grow. If hair growth is the measure of success, the child may be set up for failure. For example, a child can do really well for weeks, then have a setback and pull out most of the new growth. A person could look at the child's scalp and say, "You are doing poorly and not making progress," when the reality is that the child has been doing really well, despite one difficult episode. In therapy we often say, "Don't let a bad six minutes or six hours erase a good six weeks."

So, how does this work? A good therapist sets up a plan of action that includes all of the coping strategies identified as potentially useful and those actually being used. The child then picks a reward that he or she is willing to work hard to receive. Stickers or tick marks on a calendar each day the child uses strategies, such as wearing Band-Aids or using squeeze toys, can help. When the child has accumulated a certain number of stickers or tick marks, he or she receives a reward.

Keeping the goals short term is best, as a child will lose interest if the reward is too far in the future. Start with daily or weekly rewards, and move into longer periods as the child matures. Each reward should be age appropriate. Stickers may work well for younger children, and extra TV or computer time may work well for older kids. Some parents use fun toy rewards for younger children, such as squishy eyeballs and water snakes. Having a large repository of rewards is helpful, as it reinforces being active and can make the process fun. No matter what their age, children like to receive concrete, verbal positive reinforcement; this is often more meaningful to them than hair growth.

It is important for parents to remember that this is a process and will take some time. Many children do not incorporate strategies into their lives at the beginning of treatment. It takes time for some children to accept that strategies are needed at all. And not all children will remember to use the strategies in every situation. As parents, the more you can encourage your child to be active and to try different things, the better.

Long-Term Maintenance and Relapse Prevention

Setbacks are inevitable and to be expected. It is normal for a child to have times of success, followed by times of increased pulling. When you expect that setbacks are inevitable, they will be less disappointing, and consequently your child will feel less like a failure. It's similar to what happens with a diet program: you might do really well for a time, then for no real reason fall off the wagon and eat unhealthy foods. After a while, your motivation increases, and you get back on track. Trich works in much the same way. Sometimes there is no specific reason why a child increases pulling; it just seems to happen.

That being said, there are predictable times that hair pulling seems to increase and decrease for kids. During summer and other school breaks, hair pulling tends to improve. The lack of school pressure and homework may be partly responsible for this improvement. In addition, there is much less sedentary time during the summer. Children are not required to sit for six hours a day in classes and then need to sit for hours more after school doing homework. Summertime is filled with sensory stimulation; heat to air-conditioning, running around outside, swimming, playing, camping—just to name a few. Predictable times of setback include going back to school in the fall (sitting for long periods again) and midterms and final exam times. Also, it is important to be mindful of transitions, such as changing schools, moving to a new town, and family changes. Prepare your child for times that may be difficult.

Not all children are this predictable. Some youngsters do better with the structure of school and tend to relapse during winter and summer break when there is more free time and less structure in the day. Know your child and his or her pattern of behavior so that you can help him or her to prepare for the times that might be difficult.

Slips Versus Relapses

The relapse prevention literature makes clear distinctions between a slip and a relapse. A slip is a temporary return to a previous behavior—that is, pulling a few hairs after having a period of no pulling. A relapse, on the other hand, is a return to the previous level of functioning—that is, going back to regular intervals of pulling without the use of coping strategies. Parents should keep in mind that slips are normal and to be expected. The goal of treatment is to try to prevent a slip from turning into a relapse. When a slip occurs, handle it with care and finesse to prevent the dreaded relapse from following.

How do you do this? When a slip happens, it is helpful to encourage your child to take an investigative approach. He or she may need to ask key questions in a problem-solving manner. Questions might include the following:

- When did it happen?
- What was different about this situation?
- What strategies did I use?
- What strategies could I have used?
- What might I do differently next time?
- Has something changed?
- Do I need to alter my coping strategies in certain situations?
- Finally, what did I learn from this experience?

The last question is perhaps the most important. Your child can use a slip as a learning experience, one that will lead to better coping in the future. It may be helpful to refocus your child on goals and strategies, empathize with your child, and provide support. A response to a child who has just had a slip might go like this: "This is *so* hard! I know that you have really been working on this and it feels terrible when you have a setback. If you could rewind and do this day over, what would you do differently? If there is anything that I can do to help, just let me know."

Remember, we have all experienced setbacks in behavior change, and this is no different. Pay attention to how you feel; your child will sense your feelings and might take responsibility for them. Stay positive and solution focused, and your child will get back on track much faster. Managing trich is a process, a journey that has ups and downs. Ride the ups and downs like a car on the road. Treat each setback as a learning opportunity, and your child will learn to do the same, without judgment or shame.

In sum, the treatment for trich is quite individualized. A good therapist will be able to tailor treatment appropriately for the age and unique qualities of your child. We hope that the overview of treatment has provided you with enough information to make an informed decision when looking for help. Regardless of whether or not you seek treatment for your child at this time, exploring and understanding your own feelings will be enormously helpful. In the next chapter, we will look at some important points to consider when deciding how to move forward.

8

How to Help, Not Hurt

Mistakes Are Inevitable

More often than not, parents start the process of dealing with their child's trichotillomania by making mistakes. Rarely do parents bring their child to treatment and not admit to making some common errors in their approach. This section will review some general and specific suggestions to help you successfully assist your child with hair pulling and, more importantly, to help him or her grow and develop as a healthy, emotionally strong child.

Loving Acceptance

Probably the most important thing you can do to help your child is to love and accept him or her for who your child is, regardless of the hair pulling. Hair pulling is not life threatening (unless your child eats large quantities of hair) and is not a sign of any kind of deep-rooted problem. You must keep some perspective about the behavior, or it can become the center of a disastrous situation for the entire family. When you do, you may experience what Stu and Karen did: when they focused on accepting and loving Sarah with trichotillomania, she became able to accept and love herself.

Accepting your child with trichotillomania is probably the single most important thing you can do. This involves work for you. Recognize your negative behaviors (comments, looks, sighs, emotional withdrawal) and commit to changing them. Instead of saying, "Stop it!" pledge to say "I love you" or "Can I help you?" Make sure that you comment on many aspects of your child's life other than hair. Recognize things that your child excels at, such as sports, academics, or hobbies.

Learn to take a time-out when you feel frustrated or angry; see a therapist or talk to a friend when you are feeling down or at wits end. When we take care of our own needs, we generally feel better, have more internal resources, and increase our ability to handle difficulties. In addition, it provides a wonderful model for our children. In sum, it is your job to remain positive during this time of frustration and helplessness, which is not an easy task.

Sometimes it is helpful to ask, "What do I ultimately want for my child?" When you ask this, the answer may point you in the direction you need to go. If the answer is "To be an emotionally strong person who is confident and likes herself," then your job is to engage in behaviors that will promote emotional strength, confidence, and self-esteem. Being negative and critical goes directly against these stated goals. Now, if your answer is "I want her to stop pulling her hair," you may need to reevaluate your expectations of what is important for your child.

Evaluate Your Assumptions

Sometimes we are operating under assumptions that we do not even realize are there. For example, does having hair, eyelashes, or eyebrows lead to happiness? Do you secretly have a belief that if your child is lacking any of these he or she will not be a happy person? Are there not plenty of people out there with full heads of hair that suffer from depression or unhappiness? Sometimes we as parents have to check in with our assumptions and fears to dispel them.

This happened recently when a client attend a regional TLC workshop for teens with trich. This mother had been very calm and loving with regard to trich, until things got worse and the pulling was quite noticeable. She had all kinds of fears about what severe pulling would mean for her child in both the present and the future. More importantly, she feared that people with more severe trich were different from her child and may not be a good influence. She had unspoken assumptions about the type of people—both parents and children—she would encounter at the workshop.

We received an email from her after the first evening of the workshop. She was surprised and delighted not only with the other teens (and how precious they were), but also with the loving and wonderful parents she met. In her email, she wrote, "The girls were so sweet and normal!" This example also highlights the importance of meeting children with trich and their parents. The TLC offers numerous activities each year around the country to facilitate education, growth, and acceptance.

Educate Yourself—And Possibly Your Child

The fact that you are reading this book shows that you are doing some excellent self-study. If your child is open to talking about trich, you may want to explore some information with him or her. For example, facts you may want to share with your child are as follows:

- Having trich does not mean that you are weird or unusual.
- Trich is common.
- Trich is just like nail biting or nail picking.
- Many kids pull out their hair.
- Trich is treatable.
- There is help available.

As stated in the above section, one amazing thing you can do for your child is to take him or her to a TLC conference or retreat where the whole family can learn about trich and be with others who have similar experiences. This kind of intensive experience can foster self-acceptance and may encourage readiness for change in children and parents. It also allows you and your child to meet some wonderful people who have something in common with you.

Your child may not yet be open to talking about trich. That's fine. You may still want to educate yourself or simply to talk to your child about what you have learned so far. Leaving some reading material around the house may also be useful. Sometimes it feels too "weird" to talk to a parent about trich. In this day of computers and Internet resources, you can provide your child with good information from respected websites, such as the TLC's (www.trich.org). This will allow your child to educate himself or herself in a manner that is not intimidating.

Who Exactly Is Ready—You or Your Child?

It is often important to assess your child's willingness to enter therapy or even to work on changing his or her behavior. Not all children, especially adolescents, are ready to begin this process of behavior change by entering therapy or talking about hair pulling. More importantly, some parents can reach a point of readiness far earlier than their children. Be careful not to push your child to change when he or she is not at the point of readiness. All too often, pushing a child too soon results in the child pushing back. Remember, your child may not see hair pulling as a problem. Encouraging your child to come to one session to hear some information regarding trich from a professional can sometimes be a catalyst for change.

Diet and exercise is an example commonly used in therapy to help parents to understand readiness. If my husband suggests to me that I need to go on a diet, how does that make me feel? If he tells me that I would feel better about myself or might be more acceptable if I lost ten pounds, would that motivate me to change? No matter how well meaning these remarks are, they do not lead to motivating one to change behavior.

If your child is ready to enter therapy, find a therapist who is familiar with trich or, at the very least, is willing to learn about the treatment process. Many therapists are willing to study the disorder and obtain extra training. Contact the TLC at www.trich.org to find out if there is a trained therapist in your area. If not, start calling around to see if you can find someone who is willing to learn.

Also, be willing to learn about yourself through the therapy process. You can, and should, learn about yourself, your reactions to your child's hair pulling, and specific ways to be helpful. Sometimes parents get therapy alone long before they bring their child into the therapist's office. Improving your reactions, your perspective, and your attitude toward your child is one of the keys to your child's recovery from trich.

Unfortunately, in many parts of the country, there are no therapists familiar with trichotillomania and its treatment. If you live in one of these areas, a few resources are still available to you. Some children and families benefit from using the book *The Hair Pulling "Habit" and You: How to Solve the Trichotillomania Puzzle.* This self-help book is written for children and adolescents in a very easy-to-follow manner. It uses the model for treatment discussed in this book. Sometimes therapists find this book very helpful as well.

If using a book does not work for you or your child, www. stoppulling.com can provide information, guidance, suggestions, and feedback on progress. For children who are computer users, this website helps the child track pulling behaviors and guides him or her to choose appropriate strategies for change. It also provides visual feedback, graphs reflecting progress, and many useful suggestions.

This Is a Process. Be Patient and Understanding

Another very important thing to know about having a child with trich is that the process of managing hair pulling is just that—a process. Many people with trich who learn to cope with urges think, *Okay, I'm done. No need to worry about that anymore.* Well, the truth is that, without consistent follow-up and attention, many children relapse. As stated in chapter seven, relapse may often occur at times of stress or change. Typical times include changing schools, going to college, ending or beginning a semester, moving to another city or state, or significant family changes. Change or stress does not guarantee that relapse will occur, but it is important to be prepared and to prepare your child.

We often explain to clients that management of hair pulling is much like management of weight. If I go on a diet and exercise program and lose forty pounds in six months, I do not then go back to eating whatever I want and become sedentary again. If I do, what will happen? I will gain all of my weight back. The same idea applies to trich. A person cannot get pulling under control and then step back and forget all about it; he or she must continue with the program. Much like the weight management scenario, it gets easier and easier to "maintain," but the child must stay aware and stay alert.

After a person has gotten pulling under control, it is still important to use strategies, identify high-risk situations, anticipate difficult times, and set goals for using appropriate strategies, Managing trichotillomania is a process that must be incorporated into daily life, as opposed to a goal that will be reached, completed—and forgotten.

When and How Do I Get Involved?

One of the most common questions parents ask is "How can I help my child?" The answer has everything to do with your child and his or her individual wishes. In therapy we always ask children what *they* think would be helpful. Sometimes children do not want their parents to say anything about their hair—not to check on progress, not to nag, and not to recommend strategies for them to use. Often children try "going it alone" in this way and then decide they need some kind of help. It's important to be flexible—to allow your child to change his or her mind about how involved you might be from week to week until you discover a process that works for you and your child. If your child has tried the "going it alone" route and then decided that it does not work for him or her, consider how powerful that is. Your child is realizing how much he or she needs you. This is far more effective than you telling your child from the start that he or she can't do it alone and inserting yourself into the "solution" before your child is ready for you to be there.

Sometimes children ask their parents to help them become aware of when they are pulling or at risk of pulling. Some come up with secret phrases or secret signals that indicate the need to be alert to hair pulling. Let your child be the author of these phrases or signals, if he or she is interested. Be careful to use these phrases and signals in discreet ways, to avoid shaming or humiliating your child.

Often children like to put a sticker on the calendar that represents how they did that day. If they used their coping strategies in high-risk situations, they might get a sticker that says "Awesome!" If the day was hard, they might get a "Keep on trying!" sticker. Allow your child to craft the sticker process and to develop the meaning for the different stickers. This will encourage the use of strategies and eventually will lead to more effective management of hair pulling.

Finally, many times parents feel the need to change their child. Having a child with trichotillomania is uniquely challenging. Parents may feel as if they are doing a poor job of parenting due to their child's hair pulling. As a result, some parents are anxious and too forceful about change for their child. This can be extremely hard on the child, the parents, and the entire family. It may be most helpful to allow your child to be who he or she is. Rejoice in your child's strengths and celebrate his or her abilities. Accept this uniqueness instead of fighting against it. If you can do this, you will be able to enjoy your child and the process of parenting on a much deeper level.

Sometimes it helps to imagine yourself forty years from now. What do you want to remember about how you handled trichotillomania and your child? Likely, you want to be the person who was there for him throughout the hard times. You want to be the person who, she trusted to love her despite her struggles. You want to be the safe person who stood by him all along the way, his biggest fan, his unwavering cheerleader. Even if you did not start that way, making course corrections when necessary will be a wonderful model for your child. Be careful not to judge yourself or your child. You both are doing the best job you can at any given time. Your definition of that "best job" will change over time as you and your child develop more and better skills. The way to do start this process is to relax, accept, and love your child.

Every parent faces unique challenges in parenting. These challenges have to do with the number of children you have, their ages, your age, your model for parenting, the temperament of your child, and many other factors too numerous to mention. Add to this list hair pulling, and you find yourself in a poorly understood, isolated, unique group.

But you are not alone. In the final chapter, we will revisit the four families discussed earlier in this book and will bring you up to date on their individual journeys.

Common Questions Parents Ask

Should we tell the school?

This is a common question for parents of elementary and middle school children. The answer is "Maybe." If your goal is to have the school help your child by allowing him or her to wear a hat, use strategies in class, or to stop teasing, then the answer is "Absolutely yes!" If the goal is just to let them know without guiding school officials on how to help, then the answer is less clear. Schools want to help, but often they do not know how, so they do what they think is helpful. Without specific guidance, you may be giving information that they will unintentionally use in a way that may not help and may even diminish progress with hair pulling. If you decide to tell the school, be *very specific* about what they can do to help your child:

- Ask for permission to use strategies in class.
- Ask the teacher to let your child know *covertly* that he or she needs a strategy (the teacher can have a code phrase or discreetly walk by and hand out a strategy).

- Ask the teacher to keep a supply of strategies (that you provide) in her desk so that your child is not in class without the ability to use a strategy.
- Ask the school to educate the student body about bullying and teasing, to encourage acceptance and tolerance of differences.
- Ask for permission to wear a hat.
- Ask the school counselor to be open to your child coming in to talk if he or she needs to deal with an urge or a school-related issue.

These are a few examples of ways that the school can be helpful in addressing trich in your child. Schools want to help, but often they are uneducated about trichotillomania and how to be helpful. The TLC has great information available for educators on what trich is and how the school can help.

Should we let our child wear a wig?

When a child is at the stage of needing a wig to help to cover hair loss, the notion of wearing a wig or hair piece often arises. Sometimes parents are concerned about a wig being a "crutch." The fear is that if their child can easily cover the hair loss, he or she will never try to quit pulling. This can be true and should be considered. However, through years of clinical work, we see this question as more complex.

In our opinion, the most important thing at this point is the self-esteem of your child. If wearing a wig helps to increase his or her confidence or self-image, it is important to use one. The risk of humiliation, getting down on himself or herself, and shame from peers is not worth it. These feelings hinder the ability to work productively on hair pulling. So, at that moment, wearing a wig may the most useful thing to do with regard to self-esteem building and making progress with hair pulling.

Wearing a wig can create a much-needed barrier that can prevent pulling while the wig is on. That said, wigs are expensive and must be taken care of. If a child is not old enough to care for a wig, you will have to help with that. Further, in some cases, children pull from the wig itself. As with any strategy, it does not work the same for everyone.

9

The End of the Story

The Long Haul

So, what happens to children who learn to manage their trich? Do they stay pull-free forever? Research has not yet answered these questions. There are no long-term studies of children who received treatment for trich early in life and were evaluated in adulthood. Thus, we have no scientific research to predict what the long-term effect of early treatment might be. But what we do know is what is often reported in therapy. This chapter revisits the case examples discussed earlier in the book to see what happened to these kids down the road.

Ashley

Ashley's parents needed to understand her behavior to help them cope and eventually assist her with behavior change calmly and compassionately. Over the years, Ashley engaged in other body-focused repetitive behaviors. She started biting her fingernails at age six, and this continued until age eight. Her parents took much the same approach with this behavior as they did with her trich. They identified common situations where the biting occurred and provided alternative coping skills for her, such as handheld games and Band-Aids. This worked very well.

Over the years, it became obvious that Ashley was a very fidgety kid, and she grew into a fidgety adult. She did not like tags, sweaters, or loud noises. She slept with her soft blanket until she was twelve years old. She picked at napkins and bent paperclips, and she ripped labels off soda bottles. She did lots of things with her hands while sitting still. Although she bit her fingernails and fidgeted with almost anything, she never pulled her hair again.

Sarah

Sarah did well in treatment throughout second and third grades. She remained pull-free through middle school and high school, but had a setback her freshman year in college. Sarah had very few memories of her earlier bout with trich. She remembered her therapist and liking therapy, but not much about what they discussed.

Sarah attended her first TLC retreat as an adult the fall of her sophomore year in college. She met other young adults with trich and many professionals who encouraged her to work hard and who helped her to laugh again. About the experience, she wrote, "It was amazing to meet other people with trichotillomania! I felt so validated and happy.

I now have many friends around the country who have trich. We email daily to see how we are all doing. Sometimes we text each other if we are having a hard time or help each other out when we are having an urge. I am so lucky to have so many friends who understand me and are willing to take the time to help me when I need it."

Although Sarah has no bald spots now, she still occasionally pulls. But she is so good at monitoring her pulling that she is able to stop herself if she goes beyond ten hairs in a day. Instead of beating herself up after an episode, she takes a deep breath and says, "It's okay. Let's figure out what is wrong and make it better." Her acceptance that urges are going to happen and that she does not have to yield to them has helped her experience success. "If you ask me, I am in remission. I pull once or twice a month, but it is never more than a few. Sometimes I even giggle at myself for going with the urge instead of doing something else—it is like a game to me now."

Sarah is a great example of true management of trichotillomania over time. She has accepted that sometimes she will experience urges to pull. Instead of wishing that she would not have urges or trying to make them go away, she understands that they are a part of who she is, which helps her deal with them as they occur.

Hannah

Hannah started to pull her hair in early adolescence. She began by pulling her pubic hair and eventually moved to pulling scalp hair. Her parents, Peggy and Bob, found help through the TLC and were able to focus less on hair and more on other aspects of Hannah's life. Hannah did end up in behavior therapy for trichotillomania and self-esteem issues. She learned different ways to think about herself and about life. She became more optimistic about her future and about her ability to cope with pulling urges and episodes.

Hannah has graduated from college and is working in a large urban area. She has been pull-free since her junior year in high school. She writes,

> *I remember how mad I was at my parents for not understanding. And how mad and confused I was myself. I hated that period of time because I thought they loved me less for pulling. It felt like all we talked about was my hair! Finally, I just wanted to scream 'Stay out of my hair!' But they took the time and learned trich and more about me as a person. We all got better at handling the hair pulling. Today, I don't pull, but I still play with my hair constantly. I guess I know that it is still a possibility, but I just don't go there. My life is so awesome right now I just say to myself, 'What are you thinking? You have worked so hard to get here…don't go back!'"*

Hannah attends the TLC retreat every year and keeps up with friends in the trich world. She is an inspiration for many young people who are still struggling and has expressed interest in becoming a therapist someday. "I would love to help people with trich and other body-focused repetitive behaviors, like I got help. I want to give back because so many people have given to me over the years. I am no different from other people who pull; I just haven't done it in a long time."

Hayden

Hayden went to a small liberal arts college on a basketball scholarship. Shortly into his freshman year, his hair pulling resumed. He felt a lot of pressure from academics and athletics and from juggling the two. Hayden went to the student counseling center and found a therapist who was a good fit for him. Although no one at the counseling center knew how to treat trich, this therapist had heard of it and was willing to learn.

Hayden became aware that just as he had started pulling in high school to soothe himself around his sadness about his parents' divorce, he was soothing himself now. Again Hayden had to learn strategies to cope with feelings of frustration, anxiety, and fear of failure. Once again, he was successful.

Hayden graduated with honors and went on to get a master's degree in business administration. He is employed by a large financial firm and is pull-free. He writes,

> *As much as I hated it, I am glad I went through having trich. I think I have more empathy for people who have habits that are hard to change. I see people trying to change their diets or to quit smoking and I think…I completely understand. They are just trying to feel better…just like I was. If I have a child with trichotillomania, I*

will be there for him. I will support him because I understand what it feels like. My parents didn't know, but I will.

Moving Forward

We hope this book has been a source of good information and greater understanding of your feelings, of your reactions, and of your child's hair pulling. Our goal has been to provide information about trich to help you gain perspective and to give you strength and courage to move forward. Although trich can be frustrating, angering, and sometimes hopelessly exhausting, it can also be a turning point for you and your family.

Instead of fighting the presence of trich in your life, accept that it just *is* in your life. Once you can do that, you can begin to make positive changes for you, your child, and your family. Christina Pearson, the executive director and founder of the Trichotillomania Learning Center, once said the following, which applies to parents as much as it does to children struggling with trich: "You are not responsible for the fact that you [or your child] have trichotillomania, but you are responsible for how you approach it. You can either choose to be a victim, or learn to walk with grace." Let this moment be the beginning of your graceful journey.

Bibliography

American Psychiatric Association. *Diagnostic and Statistical Manual of Mental Disorders.* 4th ed. Washington, D.C.: Author, 1994.

Azrin, N. H., & Nunn, R. G. (1973). Habit-reversal: A method of eliminating nervous habits and tics. Behaviour Research and Therapy, 11, 619-628.

Christenson, G. A., Pyle, R. L., & Mitchell, J. E. (1991). Estimated lifetime prevalence of trichotillomania in college students. Journal of Clinical Psychiatry, 52, 415-417.

Diefenbach, G.J., Mouton-Odum, S., & Stanley, M.A. (2002). Affective correlates of trichotillomania. Behaviour Research and Therapy, 40, 1305-1315.

Franklin, M. E., Flessner, C. A., Woods, D. W., Keuthen, N. J.., Piacentini, J. C., Moore, P. S.., Stein, D. J., Cohen, S., & The Trichotillomania Learning Center Scientific AdvisoryBoard (2009). *The Child and Adolescent Trichotillomania Impact Project (CA-*

TIP): *Exploring descriptive psychopathology, functional impairment, comorbidity, and treatment utilization.* Journal of Developmental and Behavioral Pediatrics.

Golomb, R. & Vavrichek, S. M. (2000). *The Hair Pulling "Habit" and You: How to Solve the Trichotillomania Puzzle.* Writers' Cooperative of Greater Washington.

Hansen, D. J., Tishelman, A. C., Hawkins, R. P., & Doepke, K. J. (1990). Habits with the potential as disorders: Prevalence, severity, and other characteristics among college students. Behavior Modification, 14, 66-80.

Mansueto, C. S., Golomb, R. G., Thomas, A. M., & Stemberger, R. M. T. (1999). A comprehensive model for behavioral treatment of trichotillomania. Cognitive and Behavioral Practice, 6, 23-43.

Novak C.E., Keuthen N.J., Stewart S.E., & Pauls D.L. (2009). A Twin Concordance Study of Trichotillomania. American Journal Medical Genetics, Part B, 150B, 944–949.

Rothbaum, B. O., Shaw, L., Morris, R., & Ninan, P. T. (1993). Prevalence of trichotillomania in a college freshman population. Journal of Clinical Psychiatry, 54, 72-73.

Stanley, M. A., Borden, J. W., Bell, G. E., & Wagner, A. L. (1994). Nonclinical hair-pulling: Phenomenology and related psychopathology. Journal of Anxiety Disorders, 8, 119-130.

Resources

Websites

www.trich.org

www.stoppulling.com

Books

The Hair Pulling "Habit" and You: How to Solve the Trichotillomania Puzzle, Ruth Golomb and Sherrie Vavrichek

The Hair Pulling Problem, Fred Penzel

Help for Hair Pullers, Nancy Keuthen

About the Authors

Suzanne Mouton-Odum, PhD, is a psychologist in private practice in Houston, Texas. She obtained her doctoral degree in counseling psychology from the University of Houston and completed her residency in clinical psychology at the University of Texas Medical School in Houston. She has treated people with trich and other body-focused repetitive behaviors since 1993 and has been a member of the Trichotillomania Learning Center Scientific Advisory Board since 2001. Dr. Mouton-Odum regularly attends and presents at local and national conferences to both sufferers and professionals. She is the co-owner and lead developer of the only interactive website for trichotillomania, www.stoppulling.com, and for skin picking disorders, www.stoppicking.com. She is happily married and lives in Houston with her husband and two children.

Ruth Goldfinger Golomb, LCPC, is a senior clinician, a supervisor, and a director of the doctoral training program at the Behavior Therapy Center of Greater Washington, where she has worked since the mid-1980s. Ms. Golomb specializes in treatment of anxiety disorders in children and adults. She has conducted numerous workshops and seminars and has participated as an expert in panel discussions covering many topics, including Tourette syndrome, obsessive compulsive disorder, trichotillomania, and managing anxiety disorders in the classroom. She also has attended the national TLC conferences and retreats since the mid-1990s. In addition to publishing articles for professional journals and newsletters, Ms. Golomb is an author of *The Hair Pulling "Habit" and You: How to Solve the Trichotillomania Puzzle*, a book describing the comprehensive treatment of trichotillomania in children. She is member of the Trichotillomania Learning Center Scientific Advisory Board. She is also happily married and lives in the Washington, D.C. area with her husband and two children.

Made in the USA
San Bernardino, CA
14 June 2014